PUBLIC FAITH:

Public Faith?

The State of Religious Belief and Practice in Britain

Edited by Paul Avis

First published in Great Britain in 2003 by
Society for Promoting Christian Knowledge
Holy Trinity Church
Marylebone Road
London NW1 4DU

British Library Cataloguing-in-Publication Data
A catalogue record for this book is available from the British Library

ISBN 0-281-05531-9

1 3 5 7 9 10 8 6 4 2

Typeset by Wilmaset Ltd, Birkenhead, Wirral
Printed in Great Britain by
MPG Books Ltd, Bodmin, Cornwall

Quotes p 89, 83 86, 92

p 709

Contents

Contributors   vi

Editor's Foreword   vii

1 Beyond Measurement: The Non-Quantifiable Religious
   Dimension in Social Life   1
   Bernice Martin
2 Measuring Church Trends Over Time   19
   Robin Gill
3 Seeing Salvation: The Use of Text as Data in the Sociology
   of Religion   28
   Grace Davie
4 Religion and Social Capital: The Flaw in the 2001 Census in
   England and Wales   45
   Leslie J. Francis
5 Addressing Complexity: A Psychosocial Approach to Thinking
   about Religion   65
   Wesley Carr
6 Interpreting Contemporary Spirituality   78
   Anne Richards
7 Is Britain a Christian Country?   92
   David Voas
8 Mind the Gap: Generational Change and its Implications
   for Mission   106
   Martyn Percy
9 The State of Faith   123
   Paul Avis

Index of Names   141

Index of Subjects   143

Contributors

Wesley Carr, Dean of Westminster (Addressing Complexity: A Psycho-social Approach to Thinking about Religion)

Grace Davie, Professor of Sociology, University of Exeter (Seeing Salvation: The Use of Text as Data in the Sociology of Religion)

Leslie J. Francis, Director of the Welsh National Centre for Religious Education and Professor of Practical Theology, University of Wales Bangor (Religion and Social Capital: The Flaw in the 2001 Census in England and Wales)

Robin Gill, Michael Ramsey Professor of Modern Theology, University of Kent (Measuring Church Trends Over Time)

Bernice Martin, Emeritus Reader in Sociology, University of London (Beyond Measurement: The Non-Quantifiable Religious Dimension in Social Life)

Martyn Percy, Director of the Lincoln Theological Institute for Religion and Society, University of Manchester (Mind the Gap: Generational Change and its Implications for Mission)

Anne Richards, Mission Theology Adviser, Mission and Public Affairs Division, Archbishops' Council of the Church of England (Interpreting Contemporary Spirituality)

David Voas, Simon Research Fellow at the Cathie Marsh Centre for Census and Survey Research, University of Manchester (Is Britain a Christian Country?)

Paul Avis, Director of the Centre for the Study of the Christian Church; General Secretary of the Council for Christian Unity (The State of Faith)

Editor's Foreword

In the West we are seeing an upsurge of interest in 'spirituality', a desire to become more in touch with the sacred, the divine, and to adjust one's lifestyle accordingly. This phenomenon can be substantiated both statistically and anecdotally. It takes many forms, but is frequently generated by a search for personal wholeness and a quest for meaning. It is often linked to concerns about the sustainability of the eco-system and a longing for peace and harmony in the world. In the bookshops, for example, material about personal development, relationships, meditation and 'spiritual' lifestyles far outstrip volumes of conventional piety or theology.

This awakening to the spiritual and the sacred stems from a sense of incompleteness, fragmentation and futility. Although it reflects a certain disenchantment with modern materialism and consumerism, it does not succeed in escaping from the consumerist ethic nor does it usually find it necessary to renounce the advantages of affluence. This flourishing of spirituality is taking place particularly in Europe and North America and other societies with a transatlantic lifestyle where the culture is at the same time both Christian in tradition and secular in ethos. It is significant that many people seeking greater depth and reality in their lives do not turn automatically to the churches. It does not occur to them that the churches have what they are looking for.

Probably many more people access the sacred and the transcendent in their lives through nature (landscape and seascape), music (not least sacred music), art and literature than through church worship. Such experiences lead some people away from the Christian revelation and towards non-theistic, often Eastern or quasi-pantheistic interpretations of the sacred. But there are countless others who linger on the threshold of the Church without actually crossing it. In biblical language, they pitch their tents indefinitely in the outer courts of the temple. Many of these people are 'not far from the Kingdom of God', but glimpse it as Abraham did the Promised

Land, wistfully and longingly and without clarity. Troubled by doubts and questions, by a sense of unworthiness, or held back by social barriers, secular mores, and a dearth of credible Christian role models, they may take many years to complete their journey to Christian faith. Faith is none the worse for having matured over the years, but many never arrive at the point of confessing Christ and committing themselves to his Church.

These numerous folk are the good pastor's familiar territory, the dedicated parish priest's stock in trade. Pastorally sensitive and skilled clergy, ministers and lay Christians have the privilege of leading some, step by step, over time, to faith and commitment. The variegated culture of spirituality constitutes the context of evangelism. It contains substantial residues of remembered Christianity, practised occasionally, especially in rites of passage (the phenomenon of common religion, so familiar to the clergy and about which they tend to be so ambivalent). It also embraces the newer therapeutic concerns for the healing of body and mind, for authenticity in relationships and community, for the integrity of the planet.

However, our knowledge of this spiritual culture, the context of mission, is extremely limited and our understanding of it is cloudy. In a word, the Church does not know what its environment is. It does not know whom to believe. Interpretations veer wildly apart. Sociologists who espouse an unreconstructed secularization theory predict the end of Christendom, the demise of the churches and the death of God (at least rhetorically). At the opposite extreme some of us fall for a 'soft', sentimental and collusive interpretation of the spiritual culture, as though the Church could engage in 'business as usual' (as many attempt to do). We have not faced the fact that social-cultural-spiritual changes demand a strenuous act of theological reinterpretation, a huge intellectual wrench for the churches, and a concerted strategy for sustained evangelization and pastoral nurture.

The problem is to know with some assurance what people believe in terms of religious faith, conviction and values (what is ultimately important to them), on the one hand, and the state of religious belonging and religious practice, both public and private (what they are prepared to do about it), on the other. If we cannot penetrate these theologically, we cannot engage with them evangelistically. An accurate assessment of these areas requires not only rigorous statistical expertise, but also an empathetic under-standing of nuanced religious identities that elude simple quantitative assessment.

The contributors to this book share, to varying degrees, some disquiet at a lack of rigour and insight in the way that some empirical surveys of religion are carried out. Most of the contributors took part, together with others, in a consultation under the auspices of the Centre for the Study of the Christian Church, at the University of Exeter in September 2001 and so have worked through the issues together. The Centre's purpose is to promote the scholarly study of the Christian Church, especially its mission, ministry and unity. Its academic base is the University of Exeter and its home in the Church of England is Exeter Cathedral. The consultation brought together sociologists of religion, statisticians, theologians and church officers. It provided an opportunity for practitioners and interpreters of empirical surveys of religion to expound and defend their methods in front of their peers and to explore together the problem of how best to assess the phenomena of contemporary spirituality. In addition to most of the contributors to this volume, presentations were also made at the consultation by Gordon Heald (Opinion Business Research), Dr Peter Brierley (Christian Research UK), the Revd Dr William Kay (King's College, London), Dr Philip Escott (Churches Information for Mission) and the Revd Lynda Barley (Head of Research and Statistics for the Archbishops' Council/General Synod).

The consensus of the consultation was that much current empirical research in religion did not measure adequately either religious belief or church attendance. Questions needed to be more carefully worded and interpretation of the evidence needed to be more subtle. Both questioning and interpretation needed to be better informed theologically. In particular, usual Sunday attendance figures were seriously misleading. A reliable picture of church attendance, at least in England, could only be achieved by taking account of those who worshipped at mid-week services, those who came to church only or mainly at major festivals of the Christian Year, and those who came for the occasional offices, such as baptism, confirmation, marriage (including the blessing of a marriage), and funeral services. Such attendance was just as truly 'going to church' as was making one's communion on a Sunday. At the time of the consultation, the Church of England was already putting in hand a more flexible method of counting actual Sunday and mid-week attendance. Although it does not include all the churchgoing opportunities mentioned above, this method has sub-sequently been implemented.

Overall, there was a strong conviction in the consultation that the Church of England (and by the same token, proportionally, the other churches) had been playing down the true extent of its actual pastoral constituency. That is in fact very substantial. In terms of the challenge it presents to the established church, with its national mission and territorial ministry, the extent of that pastoral constituency is actually massive. It should be obvious that, if you underplay your constituency in this way, certain consequences follow – consequences for mission, resources and deployment; for liturgy and theology; for the relations between church and nation, including the state and civil society.

Our aim in the original consulation and in this book can be summarized in four points.

- To evaluate some current approaches to the empirical study of religion – both its methods and its philosophical assumptions – and show that they lack theological finesse and pastoral sensitivity to people's experience and convictions.
- To show what better methods and approaches, particularly of the qualitative, exploratory, dialogical kind – that is to say, those that require hermeneutical skills – are needed to gauge the state of contemporary spirituality more accurately and more profoundly.
- To sketch what the authors believe to approximate to the true situation with respect to religious belief and practice in Britain today; to give an alternative assessment of the spiritual environment.
- To indicate in principle how, as a result of a more accurate and profound understanding of the context, the churches can engage more effectively with contemporary spirituality in their mission.

This book brings together leading researchers and thinkers in the disciplines of theology, sociology, demography and statistics. They believe that Church and society need to hear their message. They speak critically and sometimes prophetically. Their contributions are accessible in style and presentation and presuppose the rigorous scholarly work that they have done elsewhere, rather than expounding it in technical detail (they cite their academic work in journals and monographs, rather than reproducing it). They argue that sociology, statistics, demography and the study of ideas are relevant when we are shaping the policy and strategy of the churches.

The contributions can be collected under two main headings, in the form of questions, though several contributions deserve to appear under both:

How do we know where we are?

What are the appropriate methods and tools for making an accurate assessment of the state of religious belief and practice in Britain today? Several contributors weigh in under this heading.

- Bernice Martin criticizes the spurious objectivity of those quantitative methods (ticking boxes, yes or no answers, number-crunching) that do not allow for qualitative changes (differences in values and other presuppositions, of worldviews in fact) in the cultural context. She teases out some elusive pointers to transcendence in our present context that, properly understood and appropriated, can be used to activate the substantial Christian deposit that she believes is still present.

- Robin Gill argues that religious practice, particularly churchgoing, has to be measured over time. Moving pictures, not occasional snapshots, are what tell a story and enable us to see the meaning of what is happening.

- Grace Davie studies the revealing letters that visitors to the National Gallery exhibition 'Seeing Salvation' in 2000 wrote to the Director Neil MacGregor. Here we have unsolicited, spontaneous and individually distinctive testimonies to the impact of a spiritual resource drawn from the traditions of Christian art. They offer a prime opportunity for qualitative interpretation. Davie asks why 'Seeing Salvation' broke records for such an exhibition: why was it so successful and what does that say about the credibility of the secularization theory?

- Leslie Francis exposes a missed opportunity in the 2001 Census, when a question about religion was asked for the first time but in England and Wales (but not in Scotland) Christian affiliation was not differentiated by denomination. He asks what questionable presuppositions underlay this decision and shows how different denominational attachments are linked to different contributions to social capital, the investment of value, resources and commitment that people and groups make in the community and in civil society.

- Wesley Carr expounds the relevance of the psycho-social method for understanding the interaction between clergy and people, the effect that they have on each other through transference and counter-transference and how they change each other's perceptions. This approach (also dubbed action research) combines the insights of analytical psychology and systems theory. It enables us to interpret complexity in relationships, to understand what is going on in the Church's ministry and mission. A good deal of unhappiness and dysfunctionality could be avoided if both clergy and parishioners, so often at the mercy of unconscious projections, were more aware of these inescapable dynamics.

- Finally, under this heading, in the first part of my own chapter I bring out a lack of cogency in some recent surveys and I stress the need to be sensitive to the theological distinctions that arise from experience. I suggest that greater pastoral perceptiveness could enrich empirical research in religion.

The thrust of these contributions is that a more in-depth, qualitative and interpretative method – an empathetic hermeneutic of our spiritual culture – affords a more accurate picture than crude quantitative analysis. At the very least, the former is needed to complement and correct the latter.

Where are we now and how do we respond?

What assessment is possible of the state of religious belief and practice and what broad lines of response on the part of the churches are indicated?

- Anne Richards skilfully interprets 'spirituality', exposing the superficial character of much of the spirituality industry and making suggestive links with aspects of the Christian tradition, its symbols and practices. She is sensitive to the work of the Holy Spirit in unexpected places and warns against the assumption that God exists to validate the institutional church.

- David Voas examines the various demographic criteria that might be used to decide whether Britain is still a Christian country. His extrapolations of baptism and other figures for religious practice should ring alarm bells for the churches.

- Martyn Percy's essay also looks out across the generations, asking what changes faith undergoes as it is transmitted (not very effectively) from one generation to another, and looks to the future, particularly with regard to the decline in associational behaviour in various walks of life.

- In the second half of my own chapter I attempt a synopsis of what a cumulative and comparative use of empirical surveys suggests about the state of faith in our culture in terms of Grace Davie's well known duality 'believing' and 'belonging'. Perhaps the most thought-provoking finding is the appallingly low trust-rating that the Church registers with the people among whom it seeks to minister. It would be salutary to explore this further, to ask about its causes, including pastoral failure, and to review strategies to remedy what can only be a massive handicap to mission.

Several essays raise – at least obliquely – the question of how far the decline in the presence, influence and recruiting power of the churches is self-inflicted – particularly to what extent it is attributable to misguided local pastoral practices. This question could be explored further in terms of offputting baptism and marriage disciplines and insensitive application of the disciplines that the Church rightly requires; the abandonment of general parish visiting by clergy; the lack of stepping stones to full liturgical worship for those for whom it is strange or even weird; disregard for local identities and the structures that express them, etc. There is also an issue about the general invisibility and inaudibility of clergy and churches in the community, some of which – clergy going around incognito, the silence of church bells at worship time and the locking of church buildings where that is not necessary – is preventable.[1]

Altogether, the contributors bring out huge challenges, as well as promising opportunities, for the Church's mission in the present social context and cultural climate.

NOTE

1. On the theme of effectiveness in pastoral mission in a confusing culture see further: Avis, P., *A Church Drawing Near: Spirituality and Mission in a Post-Christian Culture*. London and New York: Continuum/T. & T. Clark, 2003.

1

Beyond Measurement: The Non-Quantifiable Religious Dimension in Social Life

Bernice Martin

The real and urgent question which lurks behind all the methodological issues raised by the contributors to this volume is: What exactly is the spiritual state of our apparently increasingly 'secular' society and what part, if any, do churches and Christian beliefs play in it? Statistical and other methods are put under scrutiny because, in order to hazard even a tentative answer to this substantive question, we have first to ask: What do we know and how do we know it? This latter is the oldest and most fundamental methodological problem posed by the social sciences ever since the time of their emergence as part of the Enlightenment. Commenting on the typical pitfalls into which the late seventeenth and eighteenth-century pioneers of the human sciences fell, Peter Gay writes:

> There were times when moral philosophers rose with unseemly haste from statements of fact to general laws, or, eager to cast their net as widely as possible, accepted facts with a credulity they would have spurned in Christians, or, imitating mathematicians, rashly imposed quantitative methods on qualitative experience.[1]

I contend that we are still liable to fall into these same traps today, despite our apparent sophistication, and that they remain a particular hazard for anyone seeking to understand the spiritual or religious dimension of society.

In what follows I shall defend the use of qualitative analysis, both in itself and in conjunction with quantitative methods, as indispensable to a nuanced understanding of the spiritual dimension of social life, particularly in our 'secular' condition, precisely because 'the sacred' has become so much more diffuse, differentiated and less institutionally confined than it was when the Christian churches had an unchallenged central role in social and political life.

It so happens that two major figures in the study of religion, the American sociologist Peter Berger and the Canadian philosopher Charles Taylor, have recently presented arguments which chime with Peter Gay's observations and are highly pertinent to the concerns of this volume. I shall frame my discussion around the issues they raise, including the distortions of understanding which can arise from strict methodological purism in quantitative inquiry. I begin with Peter Berger.

In a recent polemical essay published in the American Catholic journal *First Things*, Peter Berger argues that the first of two characteristic 'deformations' which have afflicted post-war sociology is what he terms 'methodological fetishism', that is, the dominance of method over content. It is, perhaps, natural that as a sociologist of religion (and something of a theologian) he takes as his illustration the study of religious belief through survey methods, though his discussion is *en passant* rather than in any depth. Any statement of belief, presented in the form of a brief proposition, will, Berger argues, be interpreted by respondents in different ways which are hard to analyse and are unavoidably misrepresented when corralled into standardized categories. Berger's complaint will not, of course, be news to survey researchers: it is a well recognized challenge which routinely requires preparatory qualitative studies to clarify the intentions and understandings which underlie assent to or dissent from formulaic propositions and, indeed, to develop the typologies of belief which such propositions attempt to code. Yet, however familiar it may be, Berger's demurral has some force. It raises the possibility that such exercises may indeed be instances in which survey research has 'rashly imposed quantitative methods on qualitative experience'.

Peter Berger's own phenomenological model of social experience – though not referred to directly in his brief essay – adds a further dimension to the objection. If what structures our taken-for-granted 'lifeworld' is not automatically visible to us precisely because it forms the archaeological infrastructure of what makes us at-home-in-the-world, then it is not always going to be readily available for conscious articulation. It follows that our most powerful motivations and orientations to what matters – Charles Taylor calls them 'frameworks'[2] – are likely to be too inchoate, too embedded in the multi-layered feelings and meanings which permeate both our personal histories and the culture we inhabit, to be caught easily in brief, cognitive formulae of belief, though they may well be triggered by experiences or symbols. These are the 'beliefs too deep for words', so to say, which invisibly structure our lives, judgements and choices and are embedded in the way we use language: I shall return to them when I look in more detail at Charles Taylor's views, to argue that only qualitative work can tease out these powerful but semi-inarticulate dimensions of our moral and religious being.

To return, for the moment, to the narrower focus of Berger's short and provocative essay,[3] Berger's basic methodological principle is simply: If a method of inquiry can only distort in order to quantify, then find another method! The implications of Berger's phenomenological position are similar to those of Taylor's analysis, that is, that these other appropriate methods must often involve a species of cultural detective work and deploy an engaged and imaginative examination of historical, cultural and theological/philosophical texts and contexts. This is, of course, a much less neat, positivistic and 'scientific' enterprise than one resting primarily or exclusively on what can be quantified.

On the dominance of method over content, Berger writes:

> In principle this could happen with any method in the human sciences; in fact the methods have been invariably quantitative. Statistics became the mother science for sociologists.[4]

He suggests that the reason for this is twofold: sociology as an academic poor relation is emulating the prestigious natural sciences in which quantitative methods are indispensable; and, the institutional funders of social scientific research – whether churches or government agencies – tend to want 'unassailably scientific' (for which, read, 'precisely measurable') data from which to develop policy. The result, in Berger's view, has been a tendency for sociologists and their statistician partners to use 'increasingly sophisticated methods to study increasingly trivial topics'. He adds, waspishly, that even these misdirected attempts to arrive at 'objective knowledge' do at least 'merit the name of science'.[5]

The reason for the waspishness lies in what he goes on to say about the second 'deformation' of his discipline. Sociology has been 'ideologized', usually in a 'marxisant' direction. Even trivial scientific objectivity is preferable to this, he feels. As a long-term defender of Western capitalism Berger, perhaps, regards his own position as either non-ideological or a necessary corrective to this leftward 'deformation' of the discipline. It is not my intention here to try to disentangle values from science in Peter Berger's *oeuvre*, or to assess his thesis of the 'marxisant' tendency in sociology, but only to use his complaint as an illustration of the chronic problem which has never ceased to plague the social sciences, not simply since World War Two, as Berger claims, but from their very inception: that is, how to reconcile the inevitably embedded value positions and the inescapably socially situated standpoints of the practitioners of these disciplines with the aspiration to scientific objectivity. It is a central issue, too, in Charles

Taylor's analysis. Here I simply want to register a caveat about Berger's use of the term 'ideology' which is, after all, a 'marxisant' term of art and focuses the problem too narrowly in a specific, largely political, disagreement. Taylor locates the problem more pervasively in the epistemology and methodology of the social sciences which have equated 'science' with a particular tradition of 'naturalistic' enquiry.[6]

Ever since the publication of his *The Social Reality of Religion* Berger himself has preached the doctrine he calls 'methodological atheism' in his work in the sociology of religion. By this he means the suspension by the researcher or analyst of his/her own religious beliefs and commitments in the role of social investigator. There are many social scientists – not least proponents of various postmodernist tendencies of thought (also detested by Berger) – who would argue that such Lockean disengagement is a rationalist fiction. Certainly, without for the moment ceding the field to a 'postmodernist' epistemology, it is easy to see how this entirely customary device for claiming the status of disinterested neutrality – 'bracketing' the investigator's convictions and material and other interests for the sake of objectivity – is a rather hit and miss affair. Critics usually point out how hugely difficult it is to (self-)monitor all the ways in which the observer's taken-for-granted assumptions can affect the definition, investigation and analysis of a problem leaving unrecognized residues of 'bias' or 'ideology' embedded in the procedures and, *au contraire*, how even imperfectly achieved disengagement can impoverish the interpretive capacities. Yet it is equally possible, particularly on contentious issues, for an observer to lean over backwards so far in the effort to eliminate traces of his/her own interests that he/she too easily accepts an opponent's rules of procedure and scale of weighting the evidence. The response of the Christian churches in this country to pugnacious (and often secularist) proponents of the strong version of the secularization thesis, such as Steve Bruce, has often been of this kind. Indeed, a point raised by contributors to the Conference which gave rise to this volume illustrates this distortion at its simplest and apparently most harmless. Accepting weekly church attendance figures as the self-evidently appropriate measure of institutional vitality has some-times led the churches to accept too uncritically the narrative of catastrophic religious decline, where a consideration of, say, the figures for occasional conformity might tell a less hard-nosed secularization story. Part of the problem is the unexamined assumption that occasional conformity is a measure of 'weak' religious commitment or, a measure of 'purely social' churchgoing rather than, say, a measure of a qualitatively different kind of religious connection: by our descriptors will our underlying valuations of evidence be revealed!

In part, this kind of difficulty is an effect of what Charles Taylor calls the 'naturalism of disengaged reason' which has dominated the social sciences and which, in his view, today characteristically 'takes scientistic forms'.[7] By this Taylor is designating a mode of thought which has tended to 'naturalize' secularist and reductionist assumptions by embedding them in the procedures and language of secular knowledge and regarding the result as a 'neutral' discourse. I shall return to Taylor's arguments below but for the moment I want to stay with the example of weekly attendance versus occasional conformity as an index of religious vitality. What this example hints at is that it is only by being alert to historical and cultural changes that shifts in the meaning and significance of particular quantitative 'indices' of religious vitality can be taken into account. For instance, the meaning of the Armistice Commemoration for generations never personally exposed to war is different from the meaning for those whose lives were directly touched by war; again, the statistics of church and cathedral tourism as a component of occasional conformity cannot be compared with any pre-war data since the activity itself only arose with relative affluence and mass mobility. Cultural change shifts the meaning and significance of particular symbols and behaviours.

In a paper on the statistics of baptism in the Church of England, David Voas documents a trend of this sort. His data allow him to trace with some precision an historical shift, from infant baptism as a near-universal ritual of societal as well as denominational membership, to infant baptism as a marker of specific (minority) denominational inheritance from both parents, to the current situation in which infant baptism is both in absolute decline and in proportionate decline vis-à-vis adult baptism which is now a marker of mature commitment. The social meaning of baptism has altered alongside its two-stage statistical diminution even though its strictly theological meaning has remained (more or less) constant. But note also that one factor affecting both the statistics and the meaning, that is, the institutional policy of the church towards the sacrament of baptism, has not remained constant. In the period since the 1960s, the point of the most marked decline, there has been a tendency for clergy to resist what Grace Davie and others[8] call the 'social service station' view of the church by raising barriers to infant baptism as the automatic civic right of 'nominal' or 'folk' Christians and restricting access to the sacrament to committed, practising parishioners. Such policies, of course, act as an accelerator of decline of that particular statistical 'index'. It is not altogether absurd to wonder in what senses the statistics of baptism are measuring the same phenomenon over time.

David Voas tells this story by relating the statistics of baptism in the Church of England to what he knows from other historical and social data about the context of change – often, of course, qualitative data. It would seem to make perfect sense for Voas to insist on the methodologically unexceptionable rule that it is necessary to find a measure which is consistent over time in order to derive reliable statistical indices. Yet even consistency is not as self-evident as all that. Procedures for recording baptism may be consistent over the specified period but the social meanings clustering around the sacrament and the ease of institutional access are not. For Voas' immediate purposes this does not much matter since it is consistency of recording which gives him confidence that the statistical trends shown by the baptism figures are not just an artefact of the recording process. This in turn allows him to adduce the changes in social meaning over time by imaginatively calling up relevant contexts. Nonetheless – and *pace* his final comments on the current failure of the Church of England to pass on the basic tenets of conventional doctrine to more than a small minority of the younger generation – it is less than obvious what precisely the baptism statistics are an index of.

The following example may clarify my point. Consider this passage from Charles Taylor's Gifford Lectures on the centenary of the publication of William James' *The Varieties of Religious Experience*. The context is Taylor's account of the way in which religious reform movements within the Catholic as well as the Protestant churches of Europe in the nineteenth century distributed a version of individualized, personal religious devotion which would have been wholly familiar to the New England sage.

> In the history of Catholic France, the moment at which the level of practice, as measured by baptisms and Easter communions, reaches its highest has been estimated to fall around 1870. This was well after the anticlericalism of the Revolution and its attempts at dechristianization, and after a definite movement towards unbelief had set in among the educated classes. In spite of this incipient loss, the apogee of practice came this late because it stood at the end of a long process in which ordinary believers had been preached at, organized, sometimes bullied, into patterns of practice that reflected more personal commitment.[9]

What this shows is that measurements, however meticulously consistent, make no sense outside a 'narrative' or 'story' which frames their significance. The raw French data for Catholic practice as measured by baptisms and Easter communions would seem to suggest that the French were less religiously committed in the middle ages or in face of the Reformation than in the late nineteenth century. In the middle ages there was no competing paradigm of meaning (though the Inquisition data on Europe's largely illiterate Christians might suggest a range of heterodox 'takes' on that paradigm which put question marks against assumptions of uniform religious socialization and which would give modern survey researchers on 'belief' quite a headache); and in the aftermath of the Reformation, to be French was to be Catholic. Yet in both these eras the currently accepted indices of religious involvement were at a lower level than in 1870 when secularism had already bitten deep. The explanation, as Charles Taylor makes clear in the quoted passage, is that these supposedly timeless minimum duties of membership only became accepted requirements through a process by which nineteenth-century Catholicism followed evangelical Protestantism in becoming a religion of the heart and created a religious formation concerned with the intimate, inner shaping of the self as expressed in ritual conformity.

Taylor is drawing here on a body of work by revisionist church historians who have looked afresh at the patterns and meanings of church involvement in Europe in the period between the beginning of the nineteenth century and a point around the end of the 1960s. Rather than seeing unequivocal evidence of a steady process of secularization – and, indeed, some of the quantified indices of church vitality rise for a time, as they do in Britain as well as France, even as the number of the 'unchurched' also rises – this revisionist history stresses the evidence of religious revival and confessional consolidation. The religious formation of clergy was overhauled and attempts to control or, at least, shape the lives of believers were stepped up. As a result church practice began to mean something different, as Taylor noted: it mirrored an inner commitment rather than being an often desultory conformity and automatic adjunct to societal membership. Otto Blaschke has recently gone so far as to propose that the period between about 1800 and 1970 should be regarded as a 'second confessional age'. The evidence presented by Blaschke and others looks beyond and behind the raw data on religious practice to factor into the picture the qualitative changes in the ways that religion and connections with a church, even loose ones, were experienced, as well as the institutional and cultural changes in the churches themselves and in their relations with the state and society.

In addition to the personalization of devotion, these historians document many processes which had the effect of embedding confessionalism in the fabric of the rapidly modernizing societies of Europe. These include denominational/confessional educational initiatives in the emergence of new mass education systems; policies of confessional endogamy; the growth of media and communications networks, including libraries, newspapers and magazines, based in confessional/denominational attempts to evangelize as well as to consolidate the religious formation of their adherents; confession-based leisure, self-help and charitable organizations; in some areas, even confession-based trade unions and political parties. Denominations/confessions in this way acted to imprint a whole confessional style on their members which, right up to the 1950s, remained widely recognizable. They were major institutional mediators of modernity and of broader national and class identities. My point here is not simply that the statistical indices of church involvement cannot tell this full story in the absence of the kind of qualitative data, and the interpretation of it, deployed by the newest generation of revisionist historians, but that this new data materially alters the story. It alters the story both because some of it is newly unearthed, but more significantly because much that was already known comes to be seen in a new light. As Otto Blaschke remarks: 'even historians who deal with religion succumb to the charm of the secularization paradigm'.[10] If you can resist bedazzlement by that paradigm the data can start to suggest different patterns.

This kind of analysis does not ignore quantification: on the contrary it uses statistical data, for example, to chart the distribution of and access to confessional literature or the numbers exposed to denominational education and so on, but this is used in conjunction with documentary data of many other sorts which are concerned with content and context and always need to be interpreted. This may range from content analysis of diaries, devotional literature, popular culture, educational materials, through to museum exhibits such as one in the Katharinen convent in Utrecht which displays a typical Dutch Protestant domestic interior alongside a typical Dutch Catholic one of the late nineteenth century. Callum Brown's work on Britain is part of this movement of reinterpretation. The furore over Brown's overstated, polemical assertion of the sudden collapse of Christian culture in the 1960s has served to obscure the other part of his thesis, that is, that denominational identity in Britain held up remarkably well up until the 1950s, despite certain uneven statistical indices of decline in regular institutional involvement which themselves even showed a brief upward blip in the immediate post-war period. Callum Brown's use of cultural texts – diaries, memoirs, tracts, magazines, interviews and so forth – as the material evidence of what he calls 'discursive Christianity' is not only a legitimate method but an indispensable adjunct to the statistical record. My main reservation about Brown's book is that he is far too easily satisfied that there are no cultural sources of 'discursive Christianity' left after the débâcle of the 1960s but to pursue this here would be to run ahead of my argument. At this point I simply want to underline the importance of qualitative historical data in the revision of what had been a rather uncritical acceptance of an unqualified and crude secularization narrative which rested too heavily on a particular, largely negative, reading of the statistics of regular worship and indices of 'membership'.

I want, here, to turn to one more commentary on the French situation to push another step further the case for the importance of qualitative analyses. What follows is a rather extensive quotation but the points made in it by Danièle Hervieu-Léger are made as succinctly as can be managed without losing the essential quality of her perception. She writes:

> By the terms of the Act of 1905, the French Republic no longer recognizes any form of worship. But it perpetuates a confessional conception of religion that defines religious community by reducing it in the last instance to an assembly of the faithful gathered for an act of worship ... It is not merely because of its historical dominance in the life of the nation that the Roman Catholic model was constituted, in the context of *laïcité* as the organizational reference of every religion. It is also because the ritual institutional construct that it embodies contains implicit reference to the ritual institutional construct of the Republic itself. *Laïcité* took on the social and symbolic force of the Catholic establishment by symmetrically confronting it with its own social and symbolic system – the territorial network of parishes; the authority figure of the schoolmaster confronting that of the priest; the representative body of the community of citizens facing that of the Catholic communion and so on ... It helps one to understand the difficulties France has in giving full recognition to Islam ... which has no central institution that is in a position to negotiate with the state. And it throws light on the problem posed by the regulation of sects in a country where pluralism can only be conceived in terms of the confessional model that organizes it.[11]

The stuff with which Hervieu-Léger is dealing here is precisely the kind of qualitative matter that cannot be dealt with by quantitative methods and, moreover, it is of the deepest and most long-lasting importance for the understanding of religion and of religion in secularity. It is what Montesquieu, that Enlightenment inventor of sociology *avant la lettre*, called the 'spirit of the laws', the invisible template of a distinctive cultural constellation, or what later French historians allude to under the term *mentalités*. A similar point about Britain or, more accurately, England, can be found in a most unlikely source (but one incidentally relevant to the Callum Brown thesis), the historian Arthur Marwick's analysis of the cultural watershed of the 1960s. Marwick argues that the British sixties (by contrast to France, Italy and the USA) were cultural rather than political, in part because the British establishment responded to the outrages of the counterculture in a typically 'Anglican' way – by being 'understanding' and attempting to conciliate and co-opt rebellious youth back into the 'broad church' of mainstream culture while also adapting mainstream culture to elements of the 'protest'. It is, of course, very hazardous to attempt to detect such deep-rooted, implicit models in culture, but without such attempts, analysts of religious change may sometimes be at risk of losing the plot.

All of this finally brings me to Charles Taylor's main argument, since the subterranean and mostly unarticulated level of culture is the concern of his masterly reinterpretation of the history of European thought, *Sources of the Self: The Making of the Modern Identity*. In that book he begins by arguing that human life and 'identity' as we understand it today, is not possible without 'frameworks' or 'maps' which orient us to 'the good' by showing us 'where we stand' in relation to it. In contemporary life we are mostly unaware of this process: it has become invisible to us and we are typically inarticulate about it. We can neither identify our frameworks nor sense how and from what they are derived. Indeed, many modes of modern consciousness actively deny the existence of or the need for such frameworks, in particular the characteristic modern 'naturalist' position which rejects all moral ontology and all transcendent reference as myth or illusion. John Gray's recent collection of essays and aphorisms, *Straw Dogs*, is a good example of this perspective – a 'naturalist', materialist diatribe against (secular) humanism with an (implicit) moral core based on concern for Gaia rather than humanity (or 'homo rapiens' as Gray calls his own kind): it is Swiftian, a fierce moral disgust with humanity without any of Swift's Christian irony. Taylor comments on how difficult it seems to be for people actually to live their own lives according to the moral logic of such 'naturalist' positions.

In a more recent essay[12] Charles Taylor calls these 'naturalizing' modern frameworks 'closed world systems' (CWS) or 'horizontal' systems because they close off the possibility of transcendent reference. Following Heidegger, he argues that such frameworks shape our 'world' ('lifeworld' in Schützian parlance) rendering certain perceptions 'self-evidently' untenable, notably religious belief and spiritual needs. The first of the 'closed world systems' he specifies, and the one which is most pertinent to our concerns in this volume, is the structure of modern epistemology stemming originally from the models of Enlightenment rationalists (notably Locke and Hume) which characterize the chain of knowledge as starting in knowledge of the self, followed by knowledge of external reality as 'neutral' fact, stripped of the various values and relevances which might compromise that neutrality. These in turn come into the chain at the third level, and only then, if they can be derived via the first and second levels. Knowledge of the transcendent is admissible at the fourth level, again validated only by derivation from the first three stages.

The epistemological picture, combining as it does very often with some understanding of modern science, operates frequently as a CWS. The priority relations tell us not only what is learned before what, but also what can be inferred on the basis of what.[13]

In relegating what Taylor calls 'our primordial predicament', including all moral and transcendent reference, to a virtually unachievable stage four, this epistemology, he believes, puts the cart before the horse. It has, of course, been extensively criticized – 'deconstructed' is Taylor's term – in the academy but this has not prevented it becoming taken for granted by a largely secularized culture at the popular level as well as in the main body of the academy. And this, indeed, is the truly extraordinary situation in the modern West to which Charles Taylor draws our jaded attention. For the first time in human history the post-Enlightenment West has made the two crucial moves which have constituted our secular age: it has insisted on a clear division between 'natural' and 'supernatural', and it has made it seem possible to live entirely within the 'natural'. Taylor's work is an attempt to explain the history of how this was achieved – and what is hidden by that 'naturalization'.

At the simplest level, Taylor's is another exploration of the relativizing consequences of pluralism: all the traditional theological and philosophical frameworks suffer relativization and downgrading once they are forced to co-exist with each other and with their many cross-bred progeny in the contemporary world. 'None forms the horizon of the whole society in the modern West.'[14] What is novel in Taylor's 'take' on this postmodern dilemma is that he shows how it affects not only those who choose to remain within traditional frameworks like orthodox Christianity, now rendered 'fragile and permeable', but also those captured by the now 'naturalized' critiques which did the damage. He shows how these secular or, more precisely, anti-transcendental critiques have obscured what he terms the 'moral sources' of the modern identity, especially the moral sources of their own positions. The result is a condition of widespread moral inarticulacy – why, after all, on his own premises, should the uncertain future of Gaia matter to John Gray? – and an incipient confusion within all of us. Both the now fragile traditional frameworks and the new 'naturalized' closed world systems work at maintaining themselves and suffer relativization. The result is that 'great numbers of people are not firmly embedded in any context, but are puzzled, cross-pressured, or have constituted by bricolage a sort of median position'.[15]

Taylor's objective in *Sources of the Self* is to tease out the mostly occluded moral sources of the modern secular 'natural' world and show how the different skeins of thought operated to constitute 'the modern identity'. He is not, of course, suggesting that philosophical arguments brought this about by themselves but in conjunction with empirical and cultural changes which gave purchase and plausibility to new ways of experiencing/interpreting the self. (Taylor himself does little more than sketch the sort of empirical changes involved here: it would be a challenging but valuable task for sociology to flesh it out more fully.)

Taylor's analysis centres on the paradox that the modern West seems to have arrived at a set of broadly accepted moral imperatives – and incidentally, though he does not discuss this, seeks to impose them globally through international agencies both secular and religious. These imperatives cluster around the dignity of the human individual and include such values as autonomy, justice and liberty, being coded today increasingly in terms of universal human 'rights'; the duty of enlarging human happiness and preventing death and suffering, that is, a universal benevolence; and the affirmation of the value of ordinary life. He reviews movements of thought from the point where the Enlightenment began to contest the Christian dominance of knowledge and concludes that the moral sources which underpin these contemporary imperatives are profoundly contradictory.

He identifies three main clusters which constitute these moral sources: the original (Christian) theistic grounding for these standards; the naturalism of disengaged reason (which itself redeployed secularized variants of Christian values such as the intrinsic dignity of 'Man' or the duty of disinterested concern for one's neighbour which could not be straightforwardly inferred from its own epistemology); and Romantic expressivism and its modernist successor visions which began in a conception of Nature as spiritual force (again, often in origin a 'pagan' or secular transposition of the idea of the natural world sanctified with the indwelling spirit of the Creator-God). Taylor plots in detail the journey taken by European thought to arrive at this juncture via three broad routes which apply equally to Christian and secular positions. These are: the 'turn inward' to the idea of a deep self within, which starts with Augustine before beginning its secular metamorphoses via Enlightenment rationalism and Romantic emotionalism; the affirmation of ordinary life, beginning in Reformation Protestantism with its emphasis on the mundane, notably work and family life, as the proper sphere of spiritual endeavour before taking a variety of secular forms and shedding asceticism in favour of expressive hedonism; and the voice of Nature, initially equated with the voice of God or the manifestation of a Providential Order, before fragmenting in secular Romantic and Modernist directions.

Taylor's summary of our current situation reads:

The original unity of the theistic horizon has been shattered, and the sources can now be found on diverse frontiers, including our own powers and nature. The fact that there is so much agreement about the standards, over deep divisions about the sources, is one of the motivations for the kind of moral theory, widespread today, which tries to reconstruct ethics without any reference to the good.[16]

The final stage of Taylor's argument is to suggest that what has enabled the current secular, 'natural', 'closed world systems' to form the core of what is now taken for granted is not the knock-down intellectual force of the materialist argument – that, after all, has been challenged on the basis of its epistemology and has been shown to contain flaws and lacunae even by its own premises – but because of the attraction of its occluded moral agenda. Most of this agenda comes originally out of a Christian universalism which was rendered immanent, rather than existing as a set of explicit, theologically legitimated standards, during the period of civic consolidation which succeeded the Reformation and Counter-Reformation settlements. This Taylor calls 'the civilized, "polite" order': its achievement was to render the 'modern moral order' not so much self-evident as so implicit as to be, most of the time, invisible and unarticulated.

Charles Taylor's argument is important in its own right for anyone concerned to understand the relationship between secular and religious 'lifeworlds'. But I want here to draw out two particular corollaries which are highly pertinent to the concerns of this volume and which locate the earlier discussion of Peter Berger's methodological arguments about the study of religion within a more profound set of considerations. The first is that we – and here I mean not simply social scientists but more particularly Christians – need to become far more aware of the effects of 'the modern epistemology', based as it is in the principles and procedures of Enlightenment rationalism, when we are conducting or drawing on the findings of social research, especially quantitative research which customarily carries the imprimatur of 'science' and 'objectivity'. We need to become more skilled at deconstructing this epistemology and noticing how it can construct the definition of problems, of what constitutes proper evidence and what can and cannot be adduced from that evidence. Perhaps we should display more of that sceptical temper introduced by the Enlightenment in scrutinizing knowledge produced by the methods of the Enlightenment.

The second implication I would draw is that Charles Taylor has explicated and identified certain crucial senses in which the shape of our Western secular 'world' displays its Christian origins. A secular Islamic or Confucian world would look very different from the one we inhabit. It is not only the immanent moral structure that is at issue here but the immanent cultural templates which exist both in directly Christian and in a variety of secularized and semi-secularized forms as the base of Western culture. What qualitative work in the study of religion needs to undertake is an exercise excavating these half-hidden and often-denied deposits of Christianity within Western 'secular' culture parallel to Taylor's excavation of the moral sources. This would include many common topics such as ideas of the self and of identity, forms of narrativity including modes of self-narration and models of heroism, and types of sensibility including responses to aesthetic forms, to popular culture, to nature, nation and universal humanity. It is important to remember that cultural templates derived from the Christian repertoire can combine and recombine in a myriad ways – think only of the derivations of the Christ figure as template of heroism, resurfacing as the Romantic genius rejected by society, the one man of integrity in a naughty world so beloved of the 'wild west' epic and the private eye genre, the innocent at the mercy of the ruthless forces of power from Ivan Denisovich to Frodo Baggins (children's literature is full of such models).

Moreover these templates, once created, are never finally obsolete but can be endlessly revisited; consider the quest for personal redemption which pervades many commercial films. Historical models can be reworked and recombined again and again. For example, as I have argued elsewhere, it is misleading to read the 1960s counterculture as only a reworking (and democratization) of Romanticism: that carnivalesque decade, which incidentally effected the young Callum Brown's conversion to secular hedonism, was shot through with antinomian motifs and visions.[17] That is one reason for my reservations about the accuracy of Brown's thesis of the total collapse of 'discursive Christianity' after the 1960s since the Sixties themselves were a variant of one strand of that discourse while the material discussed by Grace Davie in this volume is a much more mainstream continuation of discursive Christianity on the whole not couched in the evangelical form which Brown has perhaps mistakenly taken for normative. (Other reservations include a conviction that he has attributed far too radical an impact on the female gender role to feminism: after all, much (secular) feminist work has been devoted to showing how little that gender role in fact altered, despite all the noise and smoke, while Linda Woodhead, among others, has documented a mutation in, but not a cessation of, the female mediation of religion).

Let me here remind you of an important subtlety in Charles Taylor's analysis. His argument is not that we actually manage to live wholly within the 'natural' but that we seem to be able to do so. The 'naturalization' process occludes not only the moral sources but the extent to which people in fact reach for the transcendent dimension again and again, however inconsistent it may be with the common materialist, this-worldly orientation. When a child is abducted and murdered by a paedophile, ordinary folk – and *a fortiori* the popular press – reach for a moral vocabulary which positively requires divine retribution and asserts the ultimate indestructibility of the innocent victim. When disasters occur or iconic celebrities – John Lennon, Princess Diana – meet an untimely death, religion-derived rituals become the focus of mass grief and the medium for enacting hope against despair. Edward Bailey has pioneered the analysis of what one might call this diffusion of the sacred under the head of 'implicit religion' (see for example the journal of that title published by the Centre for the Study of Implicit Religion). Bruce Reed among others has called it 'folk religion' and Grace Davie has more recently called the more event-based manifestations 'vicarious religion' on the grounds that those involved appear to regard the church (which they do not normally attend) and its professional clergy as in some sense their proxies in dealing with the spiritual and the transcendent as the need arises. The church operates on behalf of the unchurched and the mysteries of how it does so seem to cause neither problems nor curiosity.

Grace Davie regards this vicarious function of the churches as a long-term deposit of that process of confessional consolidation discussed above. The point is reinforced by the fact that the churches which are its focus tend to be established or once-established churches which have been closely tied in to national and sub-national identities. In part, of course, vicarious religion gravitates towards churches because they are just there, large, imposing buildings at the centre of most communities. But there is more to this than the merely pragmatic. The historic placing of churches and the symbolic significance of their architectural styles is part of the geography of sacred space in the civic structures of the West, a feature which in itself constitutes one of those formative cultural templates or – quite literally – orientations, discussed above.[18]

The situations and events which give rise to the attribution 'implicit' or 'vicarious' religion often provide rich data – discourses and texts in the broadest sense such as sets of letters, books of condolence, rituals, artefacts and artworks, memoirs and interviews. These constitute important and under-valued data which often contain remarkably articulate and explicit clues to the normally hidden cultural signs of connection to, as well as disconnection from, the original Christian sources. We should take such material seriously and refuse to be daunted by the fear that the academy requires our analyses to take a scientific, not to say a 'scientistic', form.

What does all this mean for the churches? In the first place I think we should acknowledge the degree to which, particularly since the 1960s, the churches have become far less effective consolidators of denominational Christian identity, in particular in their declining ability to induct children into explicitly Christian frameworks and habits of church connection. The

1960s saw a sharp falling off of all the quantitative indices of direct church involvement all over Europe. That much is uncontested though it is not self-evident that this could not be reversed – such statistical trends have been reversed in the past. I have little doubt, either, that Charles Taylor is correct in his arguments about the increased dominance of the 'closed world systems' which make it seem possible to live purely in the 'natural' world; these systems are especially promoted in the academy and the higher mass media. The cultural onslaught on the ascetic and on authority in the cultural upheavals of the 1960s was a sharp reinforcement of that process and affected the churches almost as much as the 'secular' world. At the same time, however, the sixties constituted a dramatic denial of just that 'naturalizing' process in being a reassertion of the ecstatic, the transcendent and the spiritual possibility. The sixties gave a further boost to the migration of the sacred outside the churches (not just to the classical concert hall but to the rock festival, and the ecological protest, for example) and into a whole new set of often private, non-institutional contexts. In fact, it was at one level the latest mutation of the original Puritan assertion of ordinary life as the proper domain of spirit.

Underneath all this lies the original Christian deposit still partly shaping the secular forms of Western culture, even at several removes. The church needs to become much more explicitly aware of this as the context of its work. It both inoculates the mass of the population against the felt need for an explicit religious commitment (the culture mostly does it without reference to God or church and, in emergencies, the church remains the fail-safe option). Yet the Christian deposit can be activated, especially through those events which demonstrate a continuing hunger for transcendent reference and spiritual meaning. The 'naturalization' process has occluded but not destroyed these needs. They remain opportunities for the manifestation of the full Christian repertoire demonstrating the shape of an alternative 'world' beyond the impoverished 'natural' one which we mostly inhabit most of the time.

NOTES

1. Gay, P., *The Enlightenment: An Interpretation*, p. 323.
2. Taylor, C., *Sources of the Self: the Making of the Modern Identity*.
3. Berger, P. L., 'Whatever Happened to Sociology?'
4. 'Whatever Happened to Sociology?', p. 28.
5. 'Whatever Happened to Sociology?', p. 28.
6. Taylor, *Sources of the Self*.
7. *Sources of the Self*.
8. Davie, G., *Religion in Britain Since 1945* and *Religion in Modern Europe*.

9. Taylor, C., *Varieties of Religion Today*, pp. 10–11.
10. Blaschke, O., 'Europe Between 1800 and 1970', p. 1.
11. Hervieu-Léger, D., 'The Twofold Limit of the Notion of Secularization', pp. 123–4.
12. Taylor, C., 'What is Secularity?'
13. Taylor, 'What is Secularity?', p. 4.
14. Taylor, *Sources of the Self*, p. 17.
15. Taylor, 'What is Secularity?', p. 2.
16. Taylor, *Sources of the Self*, p. 496.
17. Martin, B., *A Sociology of Contemporary Cultural Change*.
18. Martin, D. A., *Christian Language and Its Mutations*.

REFERENCES AND FURTHER READING

Berger, P. L., *The Social Reality of Religion*. London, Faber and Faber, 1969.

Berger, P. L., 'Whatever Happened to Sociology?' in *First Things: The Journal of Religion and Public Life* 126 (Oct. 2002), pp. 27–9.

Blaschke, O., 'Europe Between 1800 and 1970: A Second Confessional Age', paper delivered at the Conference on 'Is There an Alternative Master Narrative To Secularization?', University of Amsterdam, April 2002.

Brown, C., *The Death of Christian Britain: Understanding Secularization 1800–2000*. London, Routledge, 2001.

Davie, G., *Religion in Britain Since 1945: Believing Without Belonging*. Oxford, Blackwell, 1994.

Davie, G., *Religion in Modern Europe: a Memory Mutates*. Oxford, Oxford University Press, 2000.

Gay, P., *The Enlightenment: An Interpretation. 2, The Science of Freedom*. London, Weidenfeld and Nicolson, 1969.

Gray, J., *Straw Dogs: Thoughts on Humans and Other Animals*. London, Granta Books, 2002.

Hervieu-Léger, D., 'The Twofold Limit of the Notion of Secularization' in Woodhead, L. with Heelas, P. and Martin, D. (eds), *Peter Berger and the Study of Religion*, London and New York, Routledge, 2001, pp. 112–26.

James, W., *The Varieties of Religious Experience*. Harmondsworth, Penguin, 1982.

Martin, B., *A Sociology of Contemporary Cultural Change*. Oxford, Blackwell, 1981.

Martin, D. A., *Christian Language and Its Mutations*. Aldershot, Ashgate, 2002. Ch. 7, 'Religion and Politics in the Space and Time of the City', pp. 99–104; ch. 8, 'Changing Your Holy Ground: the Spatial Ecology of Sacred and Secular at Centre and Periphery', pp. 104–20.

Marwick, A., *The Sixties*. Oxford and New York, Oxford University Press, 1998.

Reed, B., *The Dynamics of Religion: Process and Movement in Christian Churches*. London, Darton, Longman and Todd, 1978.

Taylor, C., *Sources of the Self: the Making of the Modern Identity*. Cambridge, Cambridge University Press, 1989.

Taylor, C., *Varieties of Religion Today: William James Revisited*. Cambridge, Mass. and London, Harvard University Press, 2002.

Taylor, C., 'What Is Secularity?', paper delivered at the Conference on 'Is There An Alternative Master Narrative to Secularization?' at the University of Amsterdam, April, 2002.

Voas, D., 'A Demographic Theory of Advanced Secularization', paper delivered at the Surveys of Religion Symposium, University of Exeter, 2001.

Woodhead, L., 'Diana and the Religion of the Heart' in Richards, J., Wilson, S. and Woodhead, L. (eds), *Diana: The Making of a Media Saint*, London, I. B. Tauris, 1999, pp. 119–39.

Woodhead, L., 'Feminism and the Sociology of Religion: From Gender-blindness to Gendered Difference' in Fenn, R. K. (ed.) *The Blackwell Companion to the Sociology of Religion*, Oxford, Blackwell, 2001, ch. 4, pp. 67–84.

2

Measuring Church Trends Over Time

Robin Gill

Longitudinal church statistics are important both for effective leadership within churches and for purely academic research on trends of religious practice and belief. Yet there is a remarkable tendency among both church leaders and sociologists of religion to base claims about trends upon static rather than longitudinal data. Sometimes this is inevitable since only static data is available, but often it is not. There is more longitudinal data on British patterns of religious practice and belief than is often realized.

Two recent Church of England reports, *Statistics: a Tool for Mission* and *Hope for the Church: Contemporary Strategies for Growth*, provide sharply contrasting approaches. The first of these was written after a period of anxiety about the reliability of 'usual Sunday attendances' within the Church of England (an anxiety, as I have argued elsewhere,[1] that may owe more to a desire to disguise decline than to assess trends impartially). The second report, despite its optimistic title, offers a frank, even bleak, analysis of long-term institutional decline within the same Church. What divides the two reports is their use or non-use of longitudinal statistics in assessing trends.

Statistics: a Tool for Mission, which reported after a wide-ranging review and consultation, gave different reasons for the decision to disregard 'usual Sunday attendances': those under sixteen had not previously been included in the count; 'there is anecdotal evidence that week-on-week attendances are more variable now than in past years, and a simple average across all the weeks in the year, excluding festivals and holidays, may not adequately represent the overall attendance figures';[2] congregations at occasional offices are not included; variability within and between dioceses in methods of calculation; links with financial calculations can act as a disincentive to count attendances accurately. Most of these would be reasons for adjusting procedures rather than for discontinuing the collection of these statistics. From the subsequent commentary it is clear that the reason quoted here in full was considered to be the most important. The following specific example was given from a diocesan survey:

> Research in the Diocese of Wakefield provided a snapshot of the broader picture of numbers of attenders and patterns of churchgoing. A register of every person who attended a church service was taken over an 8-week period from October to December 1997 in 17 parishes . . . It was observed that 3,432 individuals attended a church service at some time during that period; this is 41 per cent higher than the usual Sunday attendance figure. In contrast, only 144 people (4 per cent) attended on all eight Sundays. (There were also 51 people who attended a midweek service, but not a Sunday service.)[3]

On the basis of this and two other similar local surveys, the report concluded that 'as a sole measure of church attendance, adult usual Sunday attendance no longer seems appropriate'. However the problem with this conclusion is that it introduced the comparative phrase 'no longer' when it cited only single-point rather than longitudinal data.

Bob Jackson, the author of the more recent report *Hope for the Church*, soon spots this obvious error. He argues that the fact that electoral rolls have tended to decline faster than 'usual Sunday attendances' suggests a very different picture:

> Many clergy have the sense that their people are coming to church less frequently than in the past. This can only be true globally if membership is falling less rapidly than attendance. But it is not – comparing the national statistics of membership and average attendance suggests that there has been no reduction in the average frequency of church attendance. This theory of declining frequency has arisen partly as a result of certain deaneries and churches taking register for a period of a couple of months or so and finding that more individuals were coming less often than they had imagined. From this important finding some people have made the erroneous assumption that attendance frequency must have dropped because in the golden age of the past we know that everyone came every week. But we don't know that. Only a repeat survey can establish whether there is a trend or 'it was ever thus'.[4]

In contrast to *Statistics: a Tool for Mission*, Jackson argues that the official longitudinal statistics of the Church of England for baptisms, confirmations, marriages, stipendiary clergy, churches open, electoral rolls, Easter and Christmas communicants, and usual Sunday adult and child attendances, all show a significant decline in the 1980s and an even faster decline in the 1990s. He bluntly dismisses single-point evidence to the contrary: 'For one year only, the Church of England is able to say: "Good news, there are more of us on the *Titanic* than we thought" – but the *Titanic* may still be going down'.[5]

The point is obvious. Like must be compared carefully with like over a sufficient period of time to suggest a trend. My own research over the last fifteen years on church growth and decline has been dominated by a search for such evidence. First in *The Myth of the Empty Church*[6] (extensively revised as *The 'Empty' Church Revisited*[7]) and then in *Churchgoing and Christian Ethics*[8] I have argued that there is in fact a remarkable amount of longitudinal religious statistics available both for church leadership and for academic research. I will summarize this evidence in order of length under four broad headings: church buildings, membership, attendance and belief.

Church buildings

The great advantage of church buildings for longitudinal evidence is that their number and approximate size in relation to the population at large can be mapped over centuries. Their limitation is that simply as buildings they offer only limited indications of how regularly they were used for worship.

Although the first modern population census for Britain did not take place until 1801, there are many estimates of local populations before that date. In an area such as the City of London it is possible broadly to match the size and number of churches there with the local population a century earlier. So, on my estimates, the seating capacity of Church of England churches and Independent chapels in the City in 1700 was fairly equal and added together could accommodate about 45 per cent of the local population. However, these churches and chapels faced a very serious problem in the City (and then in many rural areas) once the population moved out to the suburbs. By 1900 there was already a plethora of empty churches and redundant chapels.

On a broader scale still, in the last thousand years the two peaks of church building activity were the Norman and Victorian ages. The two ages were also distinct. Whereas the Normans built Catholic churches, the Victorians built some Catholic churches, built and restored many Anglican churches, and built a profusion of Free Church chapels. In addition, whereas the Normans were building for a scattered and overwhelmingly rural population, the Victorians were building for a greatly increasing and rapidly urbanizing population. Unfortunately the Victorians also built vigorously for a declining rural population. As a result they left an extremely difficult legacy for the twentieth and twenty-first centuries.

Membership

One of the most influential attempts to use longitudinal data on church membership was by Robert Currie, Alan Gilbert and Lee Horsley in their book *Churches and Churchgoers*.[9] They argued that 'the membership of the major British Protestant churches fell from 5 to 4.5 million between 1900 and 1970, while the total British population rose from 37 to 53 million; and though the Catholic population rose through immigration, the number of British recruits to Catholicism also fell.'[10] On the basis of a mass of statistical evidence, they maintained that secularization could be measured in three distinct periods on the basis of membership statistics across British denominations:

In the first of these periods – that up to 1914 – they suggested that, although civil marriages increased from 2.6 per cent of all marriages in 1838 to 24.1 per cent in 1914, Protestant church membership increased from 18.4 per cent to 19.6 per cent of the adult population. Thus 'secularization may have delimited the number of church members and potential members ... but it did not greatly affect membership retention'.[11]

In the second period – 1914–1939 – civil marriages again increased, from 24.1 per cent to 29 per cent, but Protestant church membership fell from 19.6 per cent to 15.4 per cent. 'In other words, a rise in about a fifth in the civil-marriage rate accompanied a fall of about a fifth in Protestant density; and it seems probable that during this period, secularization, as measured by the civil marriage-rate, had begun to affect the behaviour of both church members and potential church members'.[12]

In the third period secularization became most evident:

> After 1940, the loyalty of church members' children began to fall significantly and this development can perhaps be associated with a more rapid secularization of British culture. Furthermore, from 1940 onwards fluctuations in church membership seem to become quite closely connected with fluctuations in support for explicitly secularist organizations ... during this period the short-term increase of rationalists, and the short-term decrease of church members, do for the first time seem to arise from the operation of the same, or very closely connected, causes; and those causes would appear to consist, above all, in short-term changes in the level of secularization.[13]

The strength of the Currie, Gilbert and Horsley analysis is that it was based upon a wealth of statistical data, stretching back for three centuries in some Free Churches. *Churches and Churchgoers* also acted as a pioneer work in attempting to come to an objective understanding of church decline and is now widely used by social historians and sociologists alike. Its weakness, however, is that it attempted to squeeze Anglicans and Roman Catholics into an essentially Free Church category of membership. It has already been noted that Bob Jackson does talk about 'membership' of the Church of England. Yet he sometimes uses electoral roll figures to represent this membership (while recognizing their obvious limitations) and at other times he uses Easter/Christmas communicants. Roman Catholics are just as ambivalent, sometimes using 'Catholic population' figures and sometimes baptism statistics. The reality is that, in England at least, neither Church has a stable concept of 'membership' (although elsewhere in the world many Anglicans do).

Attendance

In my own work I have found that church attendance statistics across denominations make a more reliable resource for assessing trends than membership statistics. Statistics about 'average' congregations or particular congregations on a 'usual' Sunday do offer a measure of religious activity that involves people turning up to worship whatever denomination they may belong to. Of course some denominations may instill in their congregations a stronger sense of obligation than others and, conversely, some may regard monthly rather than weekly (let alone double or even daily) attendance as 'usual'. The length and timing of services themselves also vary. No comparison between denominations is exact. Yet church-going as such does represent a distinct form of activity with many similarities from one denomination to the next.

There is a wealth of data on church attendance from at least six major sources, as well as an invaluable source guide to much of the data provided by Clive Field.[14] There is the Government's 1851 Religious Census that covered the whole of England and Wales and (with more gaps and no surviving original returns) Scotland. There are independent newspaper censuses for the 1880s, and occasionally for the 1890s and 1900s. There are occasional censuses conducted by statistical societies and individuals for the 1830s and for several points in the twentieth century. There are numerous local Anglican clergy returns to bishops, Catholic records and sometimes Free Church records, with information about average or 'usual' Sunday attendances. Anglican records often start in the 1850s or the 1860s: in Lancashire they start in the 1820s, in Oxford in the 1830s, and in North Yorkshire they continue without substantial breaks right up to the present day. Furthermore, several denominations today go to considerable lengths to collect average Sunday attendances on a systematic basis. Finally, there are the churchgoing statistics for the whole of Britain compiled from clergy returns to the censuses directed by Peter Brierley of MARC Europe/

Christian Research in 1979, 1989 and 1998.[15] There are crucial gaps in the information supplied from local churches to MARC Europe: Independent Churches, perhaps not surprisingly, have proved to be somewhat elusive. For example, some of the 1979 figures were considerably adjusted both at the time and when reported a decade later alongside 1989 figures. Nevertheless, Peter Brierley's work has become an immensely valuable resource for assessing trends through gathering original data, collating research done by others and responding sensitively to changing research methods over quarter of a century.

Despite such a rich source there are some important limitations to note about using this data longitudinally to assess trends. The Brierley censuses do allow general comparisons to be made for England as a whole. So adult attendances across denominations in England dropped from 12 per cent of the population in 1979, to 10 per cent in 1989 and to 8 per cent in 1998. But how does that compare with attendances in 1851? The trouble is that double (or even triple) attendances were common in 1851 and the census itself counted attendances not separate attenders. In addition the census did not distinguish between adult and child attendances (and did not distinguish them from Sunday school attendances in the published report despite doing so in the individual returns). An educated guess is that about 40 per cent of the population were in church on the census day (Mothering Sunday) in 1851, but frankly it is a guess. Again the newspaper censuses had variations: sometimes they used independent enumerators and at other times asked churches to make their own returns; sometimes they counted morning, afternoon and evening (as the 1851 Religious Census did) but more usually they missed out the afternoon; sometimes they counted Sunday school attendances but more usually not; usually they recorded the state of the weather but sometimes not.

Obviously comparisons are best when a survey in one place is repeated a decade or more later using the same methods (the four censuses conducted by the *Liverpool Daily Post* 1881–1912 are extremely valuable in this respect). However, if like is compared carefully with like, clear trends can be detected from this data. In very broad terms it does seem that churchgoing decline began among urban Anglicans soon after 1850, among many Free Church members soon after 1870, and among Roman Catholics soon after 1960.

Belief

Some researches have also tried to use results from questionnaire surveys, with data stretching back to the 1940s, in order to assess trends in churchgoing. However, so far, results have been disappointing since there is evidence that people too often overestimate their churchgoing rates in surveys. Yet as a means of measuring changing patterns of belief questionnaire surveys have proved invaluable.

Together with Kirk Hadaway and Penny Long Marler, I compared the results of scores of questionnaire surveys of religious belief in Britain over a period of fifty years.[16] Although the questions asked about religious belief were crude, taken together the surveys suggested three broad trends: specifically Christian beliefs have declined in the general population; disbelief has increased; and minority non-traditional religious beliefs have persisted or even slightly increased. All three trends fitted more limited comparisons made elsewhere.

For example, a survey conducted on students at Sheffield University[17] in 1961 and again in 1972 suggested that decline in religious practice had been faster than decline in belief, but none the less both had declined. In both surveys, female students were always more inclined to religious practice and belief than male students, but none the less their rate declined also. Another example is supplied by the two Independent Television surveys of 1968 and 1987, reported in *Godwatching: Viewers, Religion and Television*.[18] The percentage of people switching on television to watch a religious programme had declined, from 34 per cent to 29 per cent (although it was still very much higher than the percentage of those who went to church). And, in every area of belief measured, there was a shift away from Christian beliefs.

In *Churchgoing and Christian Ethics* I also presented evidence that conventional Christian belief is declining faster among the young than in any other age group. Even in 1947 Mass Observation reported that

> both in regard to formal observances and general attitude, the younger generation show a much more critical outlook, and much less interest. Two young people (under forty) express doubt about the existence of God for every older person who does so. It is mostly the younger generation who dismiss religion with apparent disinterest'.[19]

The European Value Systems Study Group surveys of the early 1980s and 1990 in ten European countries also established such differences across age-groups. Just taking the two British EVSSG surveys,[20] the 1990 survey found that only 31 per cent of the 18–24 age-group reported that they had been 'brought up religiously at home', compared with 58 per cent of the 35–44 age-group and 82 per cent of the 65-and-over age-group. The sharpest decline in Christian belief was noted between the 1981 and 1990 surveys in the youngest age-group: beliefs in God declining from 59 per cent to 45 per cent and in a personal God from 23 per cent to 18 per cent. Disbelief also increased sharply in this age-group: professed atheism rising from 28 per cent to 38 per cent and disbelief in life after death from 39 per cent to 52 per cent. This sharp decline in Christian belief among the young is also what Leslie Francis' twenty-year study of religious attitudes amongst 11–15 year-olds established.[21]

Another important source of evidence used increasingly by historians and social scientists is drawn from oral history archives. This evidence too suggests that the twentieth century saw a sharp move away from conventional Christian belief and practice, especially among the young. Callum Brown summarizes the evidence for the period 1900 to 1940 as follows:

> Interviews show that Sunday school attendance was widespread. Amongst the Stirling archive of 76 female Protestant interviewees, 73 per cent claimed to have attended Sunday school, 45 per cent attended weekday meetings of teetotal organisations (the Band of Hope, the White Ribboners or Good Templars), 13 per cent were in church-affiliated uniformed youth organisations, and 14 per cent were in church choirs. Most of those who didn't attend Sunday school or uniformed organisations lived in rural areas where either these organisations did not exist or travel to church was extremely difficult. The sheer weight of testimony towards children's patronage of church organisations is compelling. If the level of child association was extraordinarily high, the *intensity* of their connection was remarkable. The researcher in an oral-history archive comes away overloaded with accounts of entire Sundays, and two or three weekday evenings, devoted to religious meetings.[22]

Of course, there is never an easy way of encapsulating belief, let alone 'religiosity', in a form that will satisfy both the complexities of faith and the simplicities of quantitative, or even qualitative, questionnaires. Yet questionnaires and oral interviews do suggest that, in the absence of both churchgoing and Sunday schools, a broad spectrum of Christian beliefs in any recognizable form is unlikely to persist in the general population.[23]

Taken together the trends summarized here from these four sources do suggest that Bob Jackson's concerns about the Church of England (and British churches more widely) are justified. I am convinced that church leaders do need to take them seriously.

NOTES

1. See my *Changing Worlds* (London, Continuum, 2002).
2. *Statistics: a Tool for Mission* (London, Church House Publishing, 2000), p. 18.
3. *Statistics: a Tool for Mission*, p. 19.

4. Bob Jackson, *Hope for the Church: Contemporary Strategies for Growth* (London, Church House Publishing, 2002), pp. 6–7.

5. Jackson, *Hope for the Church*, p. 10.

6. London, SPCK, 1993.

7. Aldershot, Hants, Ashgate, 2003.

8. Cambridge, Cambridge University Press, 1999.

9. Robert Currie, Alan Gilbert and Lee Horsley, *Churches and Churchgoers: Patterns of Church Growth in the British Isles Since 1700* (Cambridge, Cambridge University Press, 1977).

10. *Churches and Churchgoers*, pp. 99–100.

11. *Churches and Churchgoers*, p. 100.

12. *Churches and Churchgoers*, p. 101.

13. *Churches and Churchgoers*, p. 101.

14. Field, C. D., 'Non-Recurrent Christian Data', Maunder, in W. F. (ed.), *Reviews of United Kingdom Statistical Sources, Vol. XX, Religion*, Royal Statistical Society and Economic and Social Research Council (Pergamon Press, 1987), pp. 189–504.

15. See Peter Brierley (ed.), *Prospects for the Eighties* (MARC Europe 1980), *Prospects for the Nineties: Trends and Tables from the English Church Census* (MARC Europe 1991) and *UK Christian Handbook: Religious Trends*, No 3 (London, Christian Research, 2001).

16. Gill, R., Hadaway, C. K. and Marler, P. L., 'Is Religious Belief Declining in Britain?', in *Journal for the Scientific Study of Religion* 37:3 (1998), pp. 507–16.

17. Pilkington, G. W., Poppleton, P. K., Gould, J. B. and McCourt, M. M., 'Changes in Religious Beliefs, Practices and Attitudes Among University Students Over an Eleven-Year Period in Relation to Sex Differences, Denominational Differences and Differences Between Faculties and Years of Study' in *British Journal of Social and Clinical Psychology* 15 (1976), pp. 1–9.

18. Independent Television Authority, *Religion in Britain and Northern Ireland* (1970) and *Godwatching: Viewers, Religion and Television* (1988).

19. Mass Observation, *Puzzled People: A Study in Popular Attitudes to Religion, Ethics, Progress and Politics in a London Borough* (London, Gollancz, 1947), p. 157.

20. See Abrams, M., Gerard, D. and Timms, N. (eds), *Values and Social Change in Britain: Studies in the Contemporary Values of Modern Society* (London, Macmillan, 1985) and Timms, N., *Family and Citizenship: Values in Contemporary Britain* (Aldershot, Dartmouth, 1992).

21. Reported in Kay, W. K. and Francis, L. J., *Drift from the Churches: Attitude Toward Christianity During Childhood and Adolescence* (Cardiff, University of Wales Press, 1996).

22. Brown, C. G., *The Death of Christian Britain* (London, Routledge, 2001), p. 140.

23. For a fuller analysis see my *The 'Empty' Church Revisited*.

3

Seeing Salvation: The Use of Text as Data in the Sociology of Religion

Grace Davie

In the Spring of 2000, the National Gallery in London, with financial support from the Jerusalem Trust and the Pilgrim Trust, mounted an exhibition entitled 'Seeing Salvation: The Image of Christ'. The exhibition became an important marker of the millennium. It was accompanied by a television series (four fifty-minute programmes on BBC2) and two handsome volumes – one the catalogue of the exhibition and the other designed to support the television series. In every sense the venture was a huge success. Over 350,000 people visited the Gallery – the largest number to date to visit any Sainsbury Wing exhibition; the television series sustained an impressive BBC2 audience (totalling 2,800,000 across the four programmes); and the catalogue outsold the Highway Code in the final week of the exhibition. The press coverage was extensive. Finally, and with particular relevance to this chapter, both exhibition and series provoked a considerable correspondence to the National Gallery – the number of letters responding to an exhibition was unprecedented.

'Seeing Salvation' set out to explore how the figure of Christ has been represented in the history of Christian art. More specifically it was concerned with the pictorial problems that the artist faced in trying to depict the image of Christ: 'deciding what Jesus looked like (for we have no records), how his suffering could be shown not just as personal but cosmic, how his human and divine nature could be made clear both at the same time'.[1] The presentation was thematic, each room containing paintings and sculpture associated with a particular idea: Sign and Symbol, the Dual Nature of Christ (as both God and man), The True Likeness (what did Christ really look like?), Passion and Compassion, Praying the Passion, the Saving Body, and the Abiding Presence. The core of the exhibition lay in the National Gallery's own collections; other items were borrowed for the relatively short period that the exhibition was open. The Christian message was explicit throughout the exhibition.

The critical acclaim – with one or two notable exceptions – was immediate.[2] The success of the exhibition was promoted through the press (national and local), through the television series, through church networks and by word of mouth. The effects were cumulative, leading to long queues for the exhibition towards the end of its schedule.

These facts are relatively well known, and there is no need to go over them again at this point. The problem lies in how to explain them. *Why* was this exhibition – an overtly Christian depiction of the life of Christ – so popular in what is generally thought to be an increasingly secular, or at least multi-cultural society? What, if anything, can we 'read off' from its success in terms of societal attitudes to the Christian narrative and its presentation in a public art gallery? A further point follows from this – one, moreover, which is central to the theme of this book: what methodologies might be helpful in order to understand more fully the religious nature of the society in which we live and the place of such an exhibition in it?

In terms of the substantive issues, one explanation for the success of 'Seeing Salvation' lies in the universality of the themes depicted. Clearly this was a crucial element in the thinking of those who promoted the exhibition:

> In the hands of the great artists, the different moments and aspects of Christ's life become archetypes of all human experience. The Virgin nursing her son conveys the feelings every mother has for her child: they are love. Christ mocked is innocence and goodness beset by violence. In the suffering Christ, we encounter the pain of the world, and Christ risen and appearing to Mary Magdalene is a universal reaffirmation that love cannot be destroyed by death. These are pictures that explore truths not just for Christians, but for everybody.[3]

The same point was echoed in the following article (one among many):

> The fascination of Seeing Salvation is that you don't need to share this world view to recognise the power of the paintings it contains. Whatever the intentions of the Jerusalem Trust, the exhibition leaves it an open question whether these works triumph because of their subject matter or in spite of its restrictions ... but you don't have to believe to see that there are miracles of some kind here.[4]

That is undoubtedly so. An important shift needs however to be kept in mind. In many cases these works of art were created for audiences or populations who knew the stories that lay at the heart of the Christian narrative, but who could not read. In a certain sense, therefore, they acted as visual aids to a constituency united by a shared world view but in which significant numbers of people were unable to access the written account for themselves. Modern British society reverses this situation: the population is now fully literate in one sense, but is very largely out of touch with the Christian tradition except in the broadest terms (at least that is what is generally assumed). How then was this population able to react to the 'Seeing Salvation' collection? How were they to recognize the universal themes in order to respond to them? The question is all the more problematic given that we live in a Protestant rather than Catholic culture – one, that is, rather less accustomed to the *visual* image that our neighbours in Catholic Europe.

I am not competent to answer these questions from the point of view of an art critic. They prompt, however, a series of reflections with respect to a major paradigm in the sociology of religion: the secularization thesis. This thesis takes different forms in different places, but is concerned primarily with the process of modernization and the place of religion, in all its diversity, within this. Those most persuaded by the thesis (and until recently that was the great majority of social scientists) assume a necessary and positive association between the process of modernization and the process of secularization. In other words, as the world modernizes, it will *necessarily* secularize – the connection is taken to be axiomatic. The reason why Europe, and especially Northern Europe, is the most secular part of the world is explained by the fact that modernization occurred in Europe earlier than anywhere else. Other parts of the modernized or modernizing world will from this perspective simply follow suit.

Significant numbers of scholars within the sociology of religion now take a different view.[5] No longer is it assumed quite so readily that the process that has undoubtedly occurred in Europe will take place in exactly the same way in the rest of the world. The United States, for example, is both highly modern and highly religious (on most of the conventional indicators) – an entirely different combination of factors from that found in West Europe. Hence a significant debate within the discipline: why are the two cases so different? The details of this discussion, which turns largely on the question of 'exceptionalism' (is Europe or America the exceptional case?) need not concern us here. We need simply to acknowledge the relative secularity of Europe compared with other global regions and the puzzling success of 'Seeing Salvation' within even this framework.

The 'problem' can be tackled in a number of ways. It is possible to argue firstly that the universal themes do indeed resonate whatever the sentiments or knowledge base of the population in question. Taking this view the degree of secularization within the population can simply be put on one side; the viewer will respond to the Christian work of art simply as a human being who recognizes him or herself in the situation or narrative depicted, the more so if these are carefully and sensitively explained (as they were in this case). A second line of thinking lies in the possibility that the population is not as religiously insensitive, or 'illiterate', as we had imagined; in other words that the residue of Christian understanding in modern European societies remains significant even if depleted. The same point can be developed further: a largely non-practising population not only remains more in touch with the narrative than we had assumed, it also responds positively to those who make attempts to articulate this narrative 'on behalf of' (the real meaning of vicarious) us all. Thirdly one might argue that those who enjoyed the exhibition and the programmes were not typical or representative of the population as a whole, but constitute none the less a significant group of people (one, moreover, that is frequently overlooked in public debate). This is a constituency linked by the networks of the various churches – networks that remain more intact than is often realised and which are still able to activate significant numbers of people.

Precisely these issues have motivated my work in recent years, within which a dominant theme lies not only in the divergence between patterns of religious practice and patterns of religious belief ('believing without belonging') but also in the subtle and continuing connections between the two variables ('vicarious religion'). Both themes have informed my thinking about 'Seeing Salvation'. This, however, is a volume concerned primarily with methodologies and the sources of data available to us as we try to understand the religious dimensions of modern British society. With this in mind, I intend to look at the three possibilities (hypotheses) set out in the previous paragraph in a somewhat specific way, using as my primary resource a collection of letters sent to the Director of the National Gallery both during and after the exhibition.

The letters

The letters in question were sent to the Gallery in response to the 'Seeing Salvation' exhibition itself and to the accompanying television series.[6] There were 461 letters overall which divide more or less into three categories: those responding solely to the exhibition (121), those responding to both the exhibition and television series (136) and those which primarily concern the television series (164). Staff at the Gallery tell me that the number responding to an exhibition was unprecedented, the number reacting to the television series rather less so.

The letter writers

It is possible to infer certain things about the writers of these letters simply by reading them carefully. A very large proportion, for example, were hand-written or typed, rather than word processed. This absence of technology, together with the style in which they are composed, suggest an older rather than younger constituency with moderately high levels of education. The letter writers' names confirm this impression.[7] Quite a number, however, indicate gratitude that the exhibition was free and the catalogue subsidized, revealing for some at least modest rather than large incomes. There are more letters from women than from men, and references to the press include disproportionate mention of the *Daily Telegraph*. The regional distribution (indicated by addresses) is, I think, more dictated by the location of the exhibition than the characteristics of the sample, but some writers undertook considerable journeys to visit the gallery; accounts of these journeys indicate the effort made by elderly and in some cases frail individuals. The letters responding to the television series reveal an even older, sometimes housebound audience, some of whom expressed regret that they were no longer able to travel and see the exhibition for themselves.

One point is striking. The great majority of letters come from people who either describe themselves as Christians or imply this in their comments. Within this category there are significant numbers of clergy and religious (both Catholic and Anglican). The number of women from religious orders is especially noticeable. Many of these people (clergy and lay) came to the exhibition as the result of personal contact – they were encouraged, indeed facilitated, by friends. Others came in groups, more often than not organized by churches in the London area, sometimes further afield. Several letters indicate that their writers came more than once to 'Seeing Salvation' and made a point of encouraging their friends. Sources of data external to the letters reveal that 19 per cent of the visitors to this exhibition had not visited the National Gallery before.[8]

An important limitation is, however, immediately apparent. It is *not* possible to tell from the letters how far they are typical of the visitors as a whole (460 letters represents a small proportion of 350,000 visitors). What follows must be read with this in mind. It also pertains primarily (though not exclusively) to the letters that refer to the exhibition rather than the television series.

Method and content

The number of letters was large relatively speaking; it was not however enormous. There was no need, for example, to sample the letters to get an idea of (a) the constituency involved and (b) their content. I simply read them all, several times. They were, moreover, a real pleasure to read: seldom has a piece of sociological research given me such enjoyment, though tinged at times with sadness (there are some very poignant comments). The reason for the pleasure is straightforward: all but a tiny handful were letters of appreciation and thanks. Overwhelming in their content is a sense of gratitude, mostly to the Director himself, for mounting an exhibition of this nature as a significant marker of the millennium and for doing it so well.

I started with no preconceptions or predetermined categories, but simply allowed a series of themes to emerge from the letters themselves – after a bit the ideas begin to repeat themselves. Two other sociologists shared this experience with me: Graham Howes, who had had separate access to the letters in order to prepare a presentation for ACE (Art and Christianity Enquiry), and Bernice Martin, a contributor both to this volume and to the initial conference in Exeter. We compared notes on the themes that emerged in our individual readings and our interpretation of the ideas expressed. The levels of agreement were very high.

What then can be gleaned from the text of these letters? There are different ways of organizing this material. It would possible, for example, to gather up the references that refer to different aspects of the exhibition: its format, its presentation, the audio guides (greatly appreciated), the written material and the catalogues, enabling a degree of factual comment. It is also possible to draw from the letters information about the contents of the exhibition in a moderately specific sense: which paintings/exhibits were most appreciated and why, or which parts of the exhibition attracted most attention from this particular constituency? These comments are interesting particularly if they are compared with the views of professional art critics (see below). Thirdly, a variety of more abstract themes emerged which cut across the more specific comments; it is primarily the latter that I have used to organize the following necessarily selective account. Each of the themes is illustrated by extracts from the letters themselves.

The emotional engagement of the writers is the first point to grasp. Over and over again, they admit to being profoundly moved by the 'experience' of 'Seeing Salvation', and for many the encounter was as much spiritual as cognitive. The letter writers responded to the religious nature of the exhibits in religious ways, constantly remarking not only on the paintings/artefacts themselves, but on the unusually reverent atmosphere in the gallery. Despite the crowds, the mood was more like that of a church than a secular gallery: people were considerate to one another as they shared a common and in many cases quite explicitly spiritual response to the exhibition.

> Thank you *very* much for putting on such a wonderful exhibition – it felt like going into a cathedral, and the atmosphere among the people was quite astonishing – we were all full of awe, sorrow and reverence. It was quite extraordinary – thank you very much. It made my Easter.

I have never known such a dense throng of viewers as quiet as they were yesterday. They were obviously very affected by what they were seeing. A wonderful exhibition – thank you!

I have never been to a gallery before where there was such a spiritual air as in 'Seeing Salvation'. We were led on a reflective journey into our inner most being. It was truly amazing – and you and your team have enabled others to gain from your insights, inspiration and giftedness.

One young American woman overhearing some friends and me apologised for joining our conversation but said that she was almost in tears such was the impact of what she saw.

A second theme is two-edged. Its negative side lies in a widely shared view among the letter writers that Christianity is unfashionable or *passé* in modern British society, that it is no longer part of the mainstream. The point is repeatedly made. Its positive side lies in the overwhelming gratitude expressed towards the Director of the Gallery for creating an exhibition of specifically Christian art as a marker of the millennium. Here suddenly is a major figure in the art world – part of the secular establishment – articulating values which are normally pushed to the margins. It is in this context that Neil MacGregor emerges as a charismatic figure, an almost personal guide (by means of the audio guides) who accompanies the visitor to the Gallery. The same theme recurs strongly in letters responding to the television series.

We are grateful for your courage in putting on this Exhibition at a time when society derides Christianity rather than respects it. And we are grateful that the Exhibition went to the very heart of the faith: Christ's divinity and humanity, His Sacrifice and Resurrection, and the Salvation offered by Grace and accepted through faith. We concluded that the Exhibition as a whole, with commentary and catalogue, was far more devotional than many a Sermon!

Faith and one's beliefs are so seldom allowed into the public arena these days that it was a real privilege to hear you speak in a way which, whilst unobtrusive and self-effacing, made such a marked impression on what you were saying – so thank you for all of that. I hope that you felt happy and, if such were necessary, vindicated in your decision to mount such an exhibition.

We write to express out sincere thanks for the programmes which you recently presented on television.
Your perceptive, thoughtful and thought-provoking(!) comments; the beauty and poignancy of the works of art portrayed; and the

reverent way in which you spoke of our Lord Jesus Christ, were so refreshing.

Sadly, there is so little on TV which honours God, so 'Seeing Salvation' was a joy and encouragement to us.

A sub-theme is already apparent. The Director is constantly congratulated for his *courage* in mounting an exhibition/television series of this nature in a nation more often described as post-Christian than Christian. Such comments are crucial for the understanding of secularization in modern Britain; they reveal, moreover, the sentiments of a group of people who are seldom heard in public debate, a point taken up in more detail in the concluding section of this chapter.

I, for one, am very grateful for your courage for putting on such an exhibition, and we hope to see more like it in the years to come.

Thank you sir for the courage to follow and to earth your vision and I have hungrily to ask – what next?

In addition to the wonderful artistic presentation, I appreciated your personal commentaries and the courageous and challenging way in which you applied the story of salvation to our present day situation and in our own individual lives.

Thank you very much for doing that in a medium which has so much to say on many levels and in an age when people seem largely unaware of spiritual values. You have done us a *great* service, as well as introducing us to some previously unknown works of art.

A third point follows from the repeated congratulation of the Director for mounting such an exhibition. The letter writers are frustrated by the absence of Christian expression in the celebrations of the millennium more generally. For them 'Seeing Salvation' filled a striking gap; more than once the exhibition was compared with the millennium dome and its very different approach to religion. By implication, there is a sharp lesson for the churches here. Are they failing to offer what an articulate section of the population clearly wants – that is, a sensitive but none the less explicit account of the life of Christ as an important and continuing dimension of British society?

I really do congratulate you and your colleagues for your great contribution to the Millennium. I will remember it all my life. Thank you for what one journalist described as your 'intelligent simplicity' in your commentary which helped me to understand as much as possible. The Exhibition was a masterpiece like Bach's great masterpieces – and such a gift to the Nation!

> I think you should also know what a tremendous effect the *Seeing Salvation* Exhibition has had & will continue to have on its viewers. It is by far the best & most worthwhile & most imaginative celebration of the Millennium I have seen.

> We are all so pleased that at least the National Gallery has recognised the true significance of the Millennium Year – what an opportunity the Millennium Dome missed!

> Deep and sincere thanks for 'Seeing Salvation' – a wonderful Exhibition with an amazing atmosphere.
> Perhaps this is the REAL 'Faith Zone' for the Millennium!

A fourth point can be found in the timing of the exhibition: not only was it held in the millennial year, it also coincided with Lent and Easter and became in this way a focal point for Lenten devotion. Up to a point such devotions occurred within the Gallery itself (they are one aspect of the particular atmosphere that the exhibition generated), but there is, in addition, considerable evidence from the letters that the catalogue was used more widely – in private devotion, for example, and in a variety of Lent/study groups organized by the churches. Dozens of Lent and Easter sermons were inspired by the exhibition (the clergy express gratitude for this inspiration, the laity likewise). Just occasionally the accounts are even more personal and reveal the tip of real distress – personal experiences are related to the sufferings of Christ depicted in the paintings. Most however speak of inspiration and affirmation, particularly where the devotional intentions of the artists were made clear in the accompanying material.

> Unfortunately we were unable to get to London to see the exhibition Seeing Salvation. However I was given the catalogue by a friend, and that alone has had a profound effect on me. The whole concept, the headings, the understanding, the insights and sheer inspiration within the catalogue have enriched my life and my understanding of God and His purposes for us, more than I can say. Each day I focus on one of the items as a start to my prayer time.

> I am writing on behalf of a group of Christian friends who independently (at various times over the past weeks) wandered into the exhibition and got so fired up with what we saw that we spent increasing time in our fellowship meetings discussing the impact the paintings had on our faith, on looking at it in old and new ways Ultimately the book *The Image of Christ* has become the main 'text' for our discussion groups, frequently grabbed and thumbed through with accompanying explanation.

A final theme can be found in the interrelationships between art and religion. Some letter writers were prompted primarily by religious motives but record their gratitude for an aesthetic as well as religious experience – resolving to return more frequently to the Gallery and to explore its collections more fully. Others move in the reverse direction: already frequent visitors to the Gallery find in the exhibition spiritual depths that were new to them. Both groups record repeatedly their thanks for the variety of aids offered to the visitor – for the written guides, for the audio guides, for the catalogue and (where appropriate) for the additional information provided through the television series.

> On a personal note I am particularly grateful how you have done so much to open the eyes of people like myself to works of art that I have not really known how to look at and understand before. I can't wait to visit the National Gallery again, don my headphones and continue my new journey into a hitherto closed world. You have enriched my life and I shall always be grateful.

> He [Kenneth Clark] taught me how to look at pictures, but you have given me new insight, because unlike K Clark, who was always very reticent about what he actually believed, you have gone into the whole series with heart and soul – something I find quite wonderful in the year 2000. Your interpretation of Titian's 'Noli Me Tangere' on the audio guide actually brought me to tears.

There were however some unexpected gaps, at least unexpected for me. I was surprised, for example, that there was *relatively* little evidence of unchurched religiosity in the letters that I read. I had anticipated more given the marked difference between belief and belonging in British society as a whole,[9] but it was not reflected in this sample. I was also surprised at the absence of what might be called 'Protestant' comment about the markedly Catholic content of many of the paintings and artefacts and the articulation of Catholic theology that accompanied these. In this respect my anticipations were quite wrong. Writers from an evidently Protestant provenance (though less numerous than their Catholic counterparts) were equally positive in their reactions – some indicating that the exhibition offered new understandings of Christian experience. What emerges throughout is a real theological awareness, not least the capacity to respond deeply to the themes of 'Seeing Salvation' and to make use of these in private and collective devotions.

It is important finally to remember that these (and indeed other) 'absences' need careful interpretation; it doesn't mean that the above sentiments were not present among the visitors to the Gallery. It simply means that these particular motivations were not those that prompted people to write to the Director.

Their use as sociological evidence

So much for the letters themselves, though much more could be said (this is a rich seam of sociological data). It is time now to look at these findings in a wider perspective and first in relation to the three possibilities outlined above. The answers in this case are relatively clear-cut.

With regard to the universality of themes, for example, there is very much more of this nature in the promotional material of the exhibition, itself echoed in the press comment than there is in the letters themselves where it is relatively, indeed surprisingly, absent. Similarly the strand that I expected and looked for (that of implicit or unchurched religiosity) was not nearly as evident as I had anticipated – there are occasional references only. Relatively few letters, for instance, indicate nominal allegiance to the churches or implicit layers of belief brought to the surface by encounters with these paintings; there are some sentiments of this nature, but not many. What was there in abundance, however, was striking and repeated evidence of a particular minority; that is a group of people who openly acknowledge their Christian belief and found great encouragement in both an exhibition and a series of television programmes that articulated the same values. And judging by the extraordinarily high attendance figures, this is a minority able to mobilize itself effectively. Quite simply they voted with their feet, not to say their pens.

The methodological context: the use of text in the sociology of religion

It is important at this point to introduce a different layer of discussion – one which resonates directly with the subject matter of this book. It concerns the more general use of text or discourse as a form of sociological data alongside quantitative (statistical) or qualitative (historical or ethnographic) resources. Content or discourse analysis is now widely used in sociology as a whole; any standard text book on methods of social research has a chapter on documentary research.[10] Such analyses take a variety of forms, ranging from quantitative techniques that measure column space or search and count words, headlines or illustrations (*content* analysis), to more qualitative approaches which read 'between the lines' and look for the implicit as well as explicit *discourse* in the text. The two approaches are frequently combined – to a certain extent I drew on both in analysing the 'Seeing Salvation' letters. Both, moreover, can be done well, and both badly.

The use of documents is not new in the social sciences; one of the most celebrated texts in American sociology in the early post-war years used letters as a principal source of data in order to understand better, and from the inside, the changes that took place in the Polish immigrant community in the United States at the beginning of the twentieth century.[11] What is more striking and more relevant to this chapter, however, is the increasing use of documents or text in the sociology of religion itself. An important illustration can be found in Robert Towler's work on the many thousands of letters sent to John Robinson after the publication of *Honest to God* in 1963. Towler's book, *The Need for Certainty* (1984), classified the reactions to Robinson's writing in a series of themes or types, each of which indicated a way of being Christian. The study permitted considerable insight into the nature of believing within the Christian constituency at a critical point in the twentieth century – the sixties indicated the end of certainty for large numbers of people.

Rather different is Callum Brown's *The Death of Christian Britain* (2001), an example of discourse analysis applied primarily to historical material. This has become a very widely read book. I would not commend all of its substantive conclusions (at least not without a good deal of qualification) but the use of text as an *historical* resource is excellent and is used to great effect to complement and in some cases to challenge the standard statistical account.

A number of recent doctoral theses are following the same methodological trend. Jenny Taylor, for instance, scrutinized a set of minutes from a government committee in order to identify the changing nature of discourse relating to racial and religious diversity in the inner cities of modern Britain. The minutes were those of the Inner Cities Religious Council;[12] they indicate a marked shift away from racial or ethnic references towards a greater use of religious terminology in public as well as private life, remembering that the inner city is a somewhat special case in this respect. This particular debate should, moreover, be set alongside the introduction of a question about religion in the 2001 census; the two issues are closely related.

Stefanie Sinclair has used the text of German parliamentary debates (at regional as well as national level) to disclose the very real ambiguities in political discussions in Germany with reference to religious education on the one hand and controversies relating to the proper dress of a state-employed school teacher on the other. In the former, the test case concerned the introduction of a new syllabus in Brandenburg (one of the *Länder* in the former East Germany); in the latter the debate pivoted on the right of a Muslim teacher to wear a Muslim headscarf. In both cases, Sinclair's exemplary analyses reveal a striking if latent

discourse beneath the text of parliamentary debate. The statements of
the politicians involved are set against the historical record and found
wanting.

Lina Molokotos-Liederman used an extensive range of press comment
not only to identify, but to understand better the debates surrounding the
headscarf controversy (*l'affaire du foulard*) in France and, more recently,
the identity card issue in Greece. Both are complex, highly sensitive
political issues. Dominique MacNeill, finally, in a series of interesting
articles, took her material from the textbooks used to teach (or in the
French case not to teach) religious education in Britain, France and
Germany. Once again subtext is as important as text in understanding the
messages that are given to children about the place of religion, both in their
own societies and in the rest of the world.

The 'Seeing Salvation' letters need to be seen in this context. They are
not unique as a form of sociological data though the content they reveal
is specific. The latter, in its turn, should be set against the very different
discourse that emerged (or more accurately might emerge if the
systematic work were done) from the press comments surrounding
'Seeing Salvation'.[13] But even a cursory reading of the latter indicates
some obvious contrasts – for example in the preferences for individual
paintings within the exhibition. The letter writers comment time and
time again on Dali's *Christ of St John of the Cross*; they also respond
positively to Holman Hunt's *The Light of the World*. Neither of these
paintings figures in the choices of the cognoscenti. The latter, moreover,
are more concerned with universal themes than the specifically Christian
content of the exhibition – indeed many of them find the latter
problematic.

A final set of methodological comparisons can be found in work relating
to other exhibitions. Patrick Michel (1999), for example, has analysed the
messages left at the exit of St Mungo's Museum of Religious Art and Life in
Glasgow (the home incidentally of the Dali). Michel's work is discussed
more fully by Davie.[14] One of the strongest overlaps with 'Seeing Salvation'
concerns the ambiguities of space when religious artefacts are displayed in a
museum rather than in their original context. Looking forwards, Sophie
Gilliat-Ray has been able to collect data on the Faith Zone at the
Millennium Dome, material that included a sample of the messages left by
visitors.[15] The analyses of her findings are not yet published but will form
an obvious point of comparison with 'Seeing Salvation' given that the two
exhibitions took place at the same time (indeed they commemorated the
same event), but were very differently conceived, a point repeatedly
emphasized by the letter writers.

Evidence for or against the secularization paradigm

One question remains to be asked. In what ways do these letters and the events to which they refer add to the existing body of knowledge about the state of religion in this country?

The debate surrounding the supposed secularity of modern Britain provides an obvious place to start, a point on which the evidence is clearly ambiguous. On the one hand the writers repeatedly congratulate Neil MacGregor for his *courage* in mounting an explicitly Christian exhibition as a marker of the millennium. This, surely, is a powerful indication that the mainstream of modern British society is *considered* secular, at least by this group of people – if this were not so, why would the Director require courage to do what he did? Conversely the acclaim that the exhibition received and its obvious popularity with the public (not only the letter writers) suggest something rather different: i.e. that there is still a place for the Christian narrative in modern Britain, even in a secular art gallery, and that significant numbers of people will not only come to see it, but take the trouble to express their appreciation in a very direct way.

The letters are but one set of data alongside many others. In attempting to assess their particular contribution, I have drawn primarily on my own work, but have kept in mind the wide variety of sources that are currently available to the sociologist, many of which are outlined in this book.[16] Taking these together, there is a general agreement that the churchgoing constituency in modern Britain is declining overall (no one seriously disputes this). There is much less agreement about how to interpret the complex situation that is emerging – one that combines the legacies of history (still able to resonate powerfully in particular situations, a royal death for example) with the increasingly diverse nature of modern living. Obligation is giving way to consumption, in religious life as in so much else, and the forms of religion that can respond to new ways of thinking or distinctive markets are the ones that do *relatively* well.[17]

Within this complicated set of mutations, some voices have been heard more than others. In the 'Seeing Salvation' letters one voice speaks out with great clarity: that of the 'traditional' churchgoing minority. This is a constituency seldom heard in public debate; I also suspect that it is insufficiently heard in church circles. Both points are understandable. Policy makers, including those responsible for television schedules, cannot ignore the increasingly diverse nature of modern Britain; nor can the churches cling exclusively to forms of religious life that younger people find difficult to understand (unsurprisingly given their absence from the pews as children).

The voice is none the less important in that it has crucial implications for decision making inside as well as outside the churches. More precisely: in their entirely understandable haste to find new markets, are the churches not in danger of ignoring a market that they already have? On the basis of these letters, the question should at least be put. That this market still exists, however, is equally clear from the 'Seeing Salvation' letters and constitutes a far more positive finding. There is abundant evidence not only of the constituency itself but of the pulling power of the network. Powerful endorsements of the Seeing Salvation exhibition passed through the churches who mobilized themselves accordingly, bringing large numbers of people to the Gallery, both directly and indirectly. Not only did 'Seeing Salvation' became a major talking point in church circles, it became a major focus of effective *activity*.

The societal debate is beyond the scope of this chapter. The popularity of 'Seeing Salvation' and the extraordinarily positive sentiments of these letters indicate, however, a group of people enormously encouraged by an initiative which affirms their values. It would be foolish, surely, for the mainstream to dismiss this too lightly, the more so in a society that is, or should be, increasingly aware of its older generations.

The last word, however, should go to the letter writer whose elegant prose sums up in four short paragraphs the essence of what I have been trying to convey:

> I read A. N. Wilson's recent article in The Spectator reviewing 'Seeing Salvation'. Thereafter I determined on a Lenten visit to the Exhibition.
>
> A friend's kindness and spring sunshine smoothed the journey from Rochester to the Sainsbury Wing of the National Gallery (being 80 + has its drawbacks).
>
> The effort involved has been repaid immeasurably in sheer pleasure, inspiration and understanding. The scholars, designers, organiser, handlers and warders of the National Gallery – not to mention the sponsors – all deserve our gratitude. I hope you will convey mine to at least some of those concerned.
>
> 'Seeing Salvation' is the only worthy tribute to a Millennium of Christianity.
>
> Nunc Dimittis.

NOTES

1. MacGregor, N., 'Introduction', p. 7.
2. By and large the mainstream press responded positively to the exhibition. Rather more critical articles appeared in the *Guardian* (Jonathan Jones, 'All things bright and beautiful', 24 February 2000) and the *Independent on Sunday* (Charles Darwent, 'How do we know he had a beard?', 27 February 2000).

3. MacGregor, 'Introduction', p. 7.
4. Sutcliffe, T., in the *Independent* Features Section (26 February 2000), p. 9.
5. See Davie, G., *Europe: the Exceptional Case* and the titles by P. Berger and D. Martin listed in References and Further Reading.
6. Copies of these letters were given to me by the National Gallery together with some additional material concerning responses to the 'Seeing Salvation' exhibition. I would like to record my thanks to the then Director of the Gallery and to his staff for their generosity and help, not least in obtaining the permission of each writer concerned to quote from his or her letter. I am equally grateful to the writers themselves, many of whom responded personally to my request, underlining once again their enjoyment of 'Seeing Salvation'.
7. The many references to husbands and wives rather than partners (the latter term is *never* used) are further evidence of an older generation; they also indicate a churchgoing constituency.
8. Data from Marketlink Research, employed by the National Gallery to survey the audiences of the exhibition.
9. Davie, G., *Religion in Modern Europe*.
10. See the titles by A. Bryman, N. Gilbert and T. May listed in References and Further Reading.
11. Thomas, W. and Znaniecke, F., *The Polish Peasant in Europe and America*.
12. More information about the Inner Cities Religious Council can be found at http://www.urban.odpm.gov.uk/community/faith/forum/.
13. There would, moreover, be a noticeable difference between the comment found in the secular press compared with the coverage in the religious papers.
14. Davie, *Religion in Modern Europe*, pp. 166–7.
15. This piece of research was carried out shortly before the Dome closed. It should yield valuable comparative material. Further information from Sophie Gilliat-Ray, Department of Theology and Religious Studies, University of Cardiff.
16. See Davie, G., *Religion in Britain Since 1945* and *Religion in Modern Europe*. Studies that penetrate beneath the surface of religious life in modern Britain are particularly valuable, for example Percy, M., *The Salt of the Earth*.
17. Davie, G., 'From Obligation to Consumption'.

REFERENCES AND FURTHER READING

Berger, P., *A Far Glory: The Quest for Faith in an Age of Credulity*. New York, Free Press, 1992.
Berger, P. (ed.), *The Desecularization of the World: Resurgent Religion and World Politics*. Grand Rapids, Michigan, Eerdmans, 1999.
Brown, C., *The Death of Christian Britain*. London, Routledge, 2001.
Bryman, A., *Social Research Methods*. Oxford, Oxford University Press, 2001.
Davie, G., *Religion in Britain Since 1945: Believing without Belonging*. Oxford, Blackwell, 1994.
Davie, G., *Religion in Modern Europe: a Memory Mutates*. Oxford, Oxford University Press, 2000.

Davie, G., *Europe: the Exceptional Case. Parameters of Faith in the Modern World*. London, Darton, Longman and Todd, 2002.

Davie, G., 'From Obligation to Consumption. Patterns of Religion in Northern Europe at the Start of the 21st Century'. Unpublished paper (details of forthcoming publication from the author).

Gilbert, N. (ed.), *Researching Social Life*. London, Sage, 2001.

MacGregor, N., 'Introduction' in Finaldi, G. et al., *The Image of Christ: The Catalogue of the Exhibition Seeing Salvation*. London, National Gallery, 2000.

MacNeill, D., 'Redefining French Identity? The Role of Religion in School' in *Religion in Modern Contemporary France* (Working Papers on Contemporary France, 3), Portsmouth, 1998, pp. 47–57.

MacNeill, D., 'Religious Education and National Identity' in *Social Compass* 47/3 (2000) pp. 343–52.

Martin, D., 'The Secularization Issue: Prospect and Retrospect' in *British Journal of Sociology* 42 (1991), pp. 465–74.

May, T., *Social Research: Issues, Methods and Process*. Buckingham, Open University Press, 2001.

Michel, P., *La Religion au musée*. Paris, L'Harmattan, 1999.

Molokotos-Liederman, L., *Pluralisme et éducation: L'expression de l'appartenance religieuse à l'école publique. Les cas des élèves d'origine musulmane en France et en Angleterre à travers la presse*. Doctoral thesis, Ecole Pratique des Hautes Etudes (EPHE/Sorbonne), 2000.

Molokotos-Liederman, L., 'Religious Diversity in Schools: the Muslim Headscarf Controversy and Beyond' in *Social Compass* 47/3 (2000) pp. 367–82.

Percy, M., *The Salt of the Earth: Religious Resilience in a Secular Age*. Sheffield, Sheffield Academic Press, 2002.

Robinson, J., *Honest to God*. London, SCM Press, 1963.

Sinclair, S., *National Identity and the Politics of Religion and Education in Germany*. Doctoral thesis, University of Lancaster, 2002.

Taylor, J., *After Secularism: Inner-city Governance and the New Religious Discourse*. Doctoral thesis, SOAS, University of London, 2002.

Thomas, W. and Znaniecke, F., *The Polish Peasant in Europe and America*. New York, Dover, 1958.

Towler, R., *The Need for Certainty: Sociological Study of Conventional Religion*. London, Routledge, 1984.

4

Religion and Social Capital: The Flaw in the 2001 Census in England and Wales

Leslie J. Francis

Introduction

The national census, conducted every ten years, provides a key statistical tool to guide major planning decisions by central and local government. The census data are also of considerable benefit to the planning capabilities of business, commerce, and the voluntary sector. When the government decided to include a question on religion in the 2001 census, this was a clear indication of the increasing recognition of the social significance of religion for matters of public life. The government, however, lacked experience in asking about matters of religion and proved reluctant to take and to accept informed advice. The consequence was that the religious question was posed in two different ways in the 2001 census for England and Wales and the 2001 census for Scotland. In England and Wales all the Christian denominations were lumped together within one general category 'Christian'. In Scotland the denominations were differentiated.

The intention of this chapter is to analyse data from the British Social Attitudes Survey in order to test the comparative value of these two different formulations of the religious question. The analysis, which contrasts the effectiveness of denominational affiliation and the single category Christian in predicting indicators of social capital, supports the wisdom of the Scottish Parliament in insisting on sub-dividing the Christian category.[1]

Religion and the 2001 census

The 2001 census for England and Wales included for the first time ever a question concerning religious affiliation. The well known Census of Religious Worship, planned and supervised by the office of the Registrar-General under the leadership of Horace Mann in 1851, was a very different kind of activity. In 1851 an official and comprehensive count was undertaken of the accommodation available for, and the actual attendance at, religious worship.[2] In 2001 a question concerning religious affiliation was included on the census form itself.

In an international perspective the inclusion of a religious question within a government census was by no means novel. Such a question has been well established, for example, in Australia, Canada and New Zealand and has been asked in Northern Ireland since the partition. In England and Wales, however, the campaign to have such a question included in the national census was initially met by incomprehension and disbelief by the civil servants within the Office for National Statistics.

The initiative to press for a religious question in the census came from the ecumenical instrument Churches Together in Britain and Ireland, from the Inter Faith Network for the United Kingdom, from the Inner Cities Religious Council, from many faith communities and from sectors of the academic community. In response to these pressures, the Census Content Working Group of the Office for National Statistics convened a Religious Affiliation Sub-group, which was invited to assess the case for the inclusion of a religious question in the census and to advise on the nature of that question. Working within the constraints of the mechanisms imposed by the Office for National Statistics, the Religious Affiliation Sub-group was required to develop an 'Indicative Business Case' for the religious question. The case was constructed in two main stages. Stage one concerned clarification of the social nature of religion. Stage two concerned discussion of the social significance of religious affiliation.

The social nature of religion

Religion remains a surprisingly emotive topic in public debate and one concerning which there is considerable misunderstanding and misinformation. The first step in the Indicative Business Case was to draw attention to the well-established academic discipline concerned with the social scientific study of religion, as represented through journals like *Research in the Social Scientific Study of Religion*, *Journal for the Scientific Study of Religion*, *Review of Religious Research*, and *Sociology of Religion*. While theology is properly concerned with assessing the truth claims of religion, the social scientific study of religion is properly concerned with establishing the personal and social correlates, contexts, and consequences of religion. Regardless of whether religious truth claims are true or not, a responsible society needs to recognize and to understand how religion affects the lives of individuals and shapes the functioning of social institutions.

The second step in the Indicative Business Case was to draw attention to the well-established distinctions made in the social scientific literature between the different dimensions in which religion is given social expression. Unfortunately, while there is considerable agreement in the literature concerning the need to distinguish between the dimensions of religion, there is no generally agreed map regarding the most economical or efficient number of dimensions, and there is no generally accepted terminology regarding the labels for these dimensions. For example, Grace Davie has done a great deal to establish in common currency the distinction between *believing* and *belonging*. According to Davie, more people believe in God than belong to the churches. In Davie's usage, this concept of belonging tends to merge with visible expressions of practice.

The vocabulary favoured by the Religious Affiliation Sub-group distinguished between three distinct dimensions of religion styled as belief, practice, and affiliation. According to this use of language, belief describes the religious formularies and doctrines to which individuals may or may not subscribe. This area is explored, for example, in the British Social Attitudes Survey by the following question:

Please tick one box below to show which statement comes closest to expressing what you believe about God:
- [ ] I don't believe in God;
- [ ] I don't know whether there is a God and I don't believe there is any way to find out;
- [ ] I find myself believing in God some of the time, but not at others;
- [ ] While I have doubts, I feel that I do believe in God;
- [ ] I know God really exists and I have no doubt about it.[3]

Practice describes the range of religious activities in which individuals may or may not engage. Two practices of particular concern to the social scientific study of religion are prayer[4] and church attendance.[5] In the British Social Attitudes Survey one aspect of religious practice is assessed by the following question:

Apart from such special occasions as weddings, funerals, and baptisms, how often nowadays do you attend services or meetings connected with your religion?
- [ ] once a week or more;
- [ ] less often but at least once in two weeks;
- [ ] less often but at least once a month;
- [ ] less often but at least twice a year;
- [ ] less often but at least once a year;
- [ ] less often;
- [ ] never or practically never.[6]

Affiliation describes the religious group with which people identify. This is a question which can be asked in a variety of ways. The broad domain is, however, indicated by the British Social Attitudes Survey in the following formulation:

> Do you regard yourself as belonging to any particular religion? If yes: which?[7]

In the British Social Attitudes Survey this question is followed by 21 options, including two write-in open-ended categories.

The third step in the Indicative Business Case was to examine the debate regarding the extent to which religion is a personal and private matter properly to be protected from public scrutiny. Drawing on the threefold distinction between belief, practice and affiliation, the following argument was advanced. Questions about religious belief, it was argued, belong to the domain of personal matters. The census should not be concerned with matters of religious belief. Questions about religious practices, like attendance at places of worship, demonstrate the interface between the personal and the public domains of religion. The very process of going out to a public gathering renders the activity open to public scrutiny. It was not proposed, however, that the census should be concerned with religious practice. Questions about affiliation, on the other hand, touch most closely the public and social dimensions of religion. If it is a legitimate matter for the census to enquire about membership of ethnic and linguistic communities, then it is an equally legitimate matter for the census to enquire about religious affiliation and membership of religious communities.

Having advanced the case for including a question on *religious affiliation* in the national census, the Religious Affiliation Sub-group faced two significant difficulties, namely the interpretation of the 1920 Census Act favoured by the Office for National Statistics and criticism of affiliation as an appropriate measure of religion.

The 1920 Census Act

The 1920 Census Act made provision for asking questions related to the 'social and civil condition' of the population. Senior civil servants in the Office for National Statistics took legal advice on this wording and made the recommendation that the act specifically precluded asking about religious affiliation. The advice reported by the Legislation Branch of the Office for National Statistics read as follows.

> There is no guidance in the Act as to the meaning of 'social and civil condition' in paragraph 6 of the Schedule, and thus the words must be

given their general meaning when interpreting the statute. According to dictionary definitions, neither 'civil' nor 'social' encompass the notion of religion. Specifically, 'civil' is defined as 'secular' or 'non-ecclesiastical'; and 'social' applies more to earthly than heavenly attributes.

The Religious Affiliation Sub-group attempted a robust response to this advice by arguing that the ruling misunderstood both the meaning of the language embodied in the 1920 Census Act and the nature of religion. On the first point, it was argued that, according to etymology *social* (from the Latin *socius*) concerns those who share affiliation in common; *civil* (from the Latin *civis*) concerns those who interact within a shared community. On the second point, it was argued that religious affiliation provides a key indicator of the social and civil condition, in senses similar to those indicators concerned with language or ethnicity.

In the event, following a concerted campaign by faith communities, the government took the option of amending primary legislation in order to ensure the legality of including the religious question in the 2001 census.

Religious affiliation

The major argument against accepting religious affiliation as a useful variable in social research is based on a failure to understand affiliation as a serious social indicator in its own right, but to see it as a poor predictor of other religious dimensions. For example, an information paper produced in preparation for the 2001 Census of Population and Dwellings in New Zealand argued as follows.

> The practical value of census information on religion is questionable, particularly in view of the fact that it does not provide an accurate indication of either the churchgoing practices of the population or the depth of a person's commitment to their specified religions.[8]

A number of empirical studies in England draw attention to the way in which affiliation is a poor predictor of practice and to how the relationship varies from denomination to denomination.[9] For example, while the majority of self-assigned Baptists may well be regular churchgoers, the majority of self-assigned Anglicans appear never to consider going to church. Herein is the problem of 'religions nominalism'.

For a question on religious affiliation to be included as a valid social indicator in the national census, affiliation needed to be understood in its own right and not merely as a poor approximation for other dimensions of religion. An important and powerful attempt to rehabilitate self-assigned religious affiliation as a theoretically coherent and socially significant indicator has been advanced by Fane, drawing on Bouma's sociological theory of religious identification, according to which religious affiliation is defined as a 'useful social category giving some indication of the cultural background and general orientating values of a person'. Then Bouma posits a process through which 'cultural background' and 'general orientating values' are acquired. Importantly, this process of acquisition is exactly the same for religious identity as it is for political or sporting or philosophical identities, and consists of 'meaning systems' and 'plausibility structures'. Bouma[10] describes meaning systems as 'a set or collection of answers to questions about the meaning and purpose of life', and plausibility structures (borrowed from Berger) as 'social arrangements which serve to inculcate, celebrate, perpetuate and apply a meaning system'. He maintains that all of us possess meaning systems from which we derive our existential purpose. He cites a living church as being one example of a plausibility structure through which a meaning system is made plausible and then disseminated. Although a self-assigned religious identity might also imply commitment to a plausibility structure (practice) and adherence to its related meaning system (belief), Bouma suggests that it might be equally, perhaps more, significant in terms of the exposure to the particular cultural background that it represents. Crucially, this alternative conceptualization avoids the difficult terrain of religious affiliation as proxy for practice and belief by recognizing that even non-churchgoers and non-believers 'may still show *the effect* of the meaning system and plausibility structure with which they identify'.[11]

The value of Bouma's sociological theory of religious identification is that it allows self-assigned religious affiliation to be perceived, and thus analysed, as a key component of social identity, in a way similar to age, gender, class location, political persuasion, nationality, ethnic group and others.[12] Religious affiliation informs our attitudes and, in turn, our modes of behaviour by contributing to our self-definition both of who we are, but equally importantly, of who we are not. This type of analysis is especially advantageous when interpreting census data, because it is inclusive of all those who claim a religious affiliation, not only of the minority who also attend church.

Alongside Bouma's theory of religious identification, Fane also draws on Bibby's theory of 'encasement' developed from his empirical surveys in Canada. Bibby argues that Canadian Christians are 'encased' within the Christian tradition. In other words, this tradition has a strong influential hold over both its active and latent members from which affiliates find it extremely difficult to extricate themselves. Contrary to the claims of secularization theorists that low levels of church attendance are indicative of the erosion of religion's social significance,[13] Bibby would argue that this trend is actually a manifestation of the re-packaging of religion in the context of late twentieth century consumer-orientated society. Consumers, as we all are, are free to select 'fragments' of faith, and we are encouraged to do this by the way in which the churches have simulated the marketing strategies of the wider society.

The central point to glean from Bibby's analysis is that the potential for religion, in this case Christianity, to be a socially significant attitudinal and behavioural determinant has not necessarily disappeared. If anything, the Christian 'casing' may have been strengthened, because the accommodationist stance adopted by the Christian churches has, according to Bibby, reduced the need for affiliates to look elsewhere.

Social significance of religious affiliation

The second stage of the Indicative Business Plan advanced by the Religious Affiliation Sub-group needed to demonstrate how a question on religious affiliation would advance the two criteria set out by the Office for National Statistics for including a question in the census. The first criterion was 'information that is required in order to implement or comply with legislation'. A relevant example of such current legislation was identified in section 11 of the Education Reform Act 1988 (as amended by the Education Act 1993). Future uses, it was suggested, would include monitoring religious discrimination.

The second criterion was information which 'would result in a benefit to the nation'. On this point the Indicative Business Case argued as follows.

The case here rests on the extent to which religious affiliation provides information about the social and civil condition of the population which is of importance for and relevance to major areas of resource allocation. Judgement on this issue hinges on the weight currently given to the secularisation thesis popular from the 1960s which claimed that religion had ceased to be a matter of public concern and had retreated into the private or personal domain. The validity of the secularisation thesis no longer commands general academic consensus. Two main sources of evidence now challenge the secularisation thesis.

First, scientific research in areas (for example) of psychology, sociology, gerontology and health care is pointing increasingly to the importance of religious indicators for predicting a range of practical outcomes. For example, international empirical research indicates the different pattern of social support required by the religious elderly, the speedier recovery rate from certain illnesses among some religious subjects, the different pattern of substance abuse among religious teenagers, and so on. Indeed, it is interesting to note that some insurance companies give significant weight to the religious variable in calculating risks. In other words, knowing about the distribution of religion within society could promote the more effective and efficient targeting of resources, and indicate the presence of fresh partners in provision.

Second, the religious communities are themselves major providers of a range of services within the community. Some of these services are comparatively overt, as for example the role of religious communities in the provision of sheltered accommodation for the elderly and hospice care. Other services are comparatively covert, as for example the role of religious motivation in prompting voluntary community services in areas like the provision of informal caring networks. In other words, knowing about the distribution of religion in society could help predict movements in the availability and provision of such voluntary initiatives, with consequent implications for the provision of statutory services.[14]

Denomination differentiation

With what seemed to be considerable reluctance, the Office for National Statistics included a religious question in the July 1997 Census Test. The pre-coded response categories listed six major faith groups in the following format.

Do you consider you belong to a religious group?
☐ No
☐ Christian
☐ Buddhist
☐ Hindu
☐ Islam/Muslim
☐ Jewish
☐ Sikh
☐ Any other religion, *please write in below*

....

Contrary to the informed advice given the Religious Affiliation Sub-group, the Christian category was not subdivided into major denominations. When the Religious Affiliation Sub-group was given opportunity to comment on the outcome of the July 1997 Census Test, once again a strong case was made for subdividing the Christian category. Six main points were advanced.

First, debate among the faith communities represented on the Religious Affiliation Sub-group recognized that the history of Christianity in England

and Wales is different from the history of the other faith groups. Generally the other faith groups accepted that their own communities should be treated as single entities for the purposes of a census question, but supported the case for the Christian community to be subdivided by denomination.

Second, if the category 'Christian' remained in the census, the main practical value of this marker to the primary census users would be to highlight the fact that these respondents are not members of other world faiths. For the practical use of census data by departments of local and central government, however, it would be important to know the denomination. For example, at the obvious level of ensuring the appropriate allocation of chaplaincies to hospitals, or of assessing the distribution of church schools, or of assessing the composition of the Standing Advisory Councils on Religious Education (for which local authorities are charged to reflect the religious composition of the local area), the denominational information would be essential. Religious affiliation is also an important predictor of certain needs for and attitudes toward health care provision, but once again it is the denominational identity which is the determining factor. For example, denomination predicts certain aspects of lifestyle and lifestyle predicts certain needs for health care.

Third, if the churches were themselves to become significant users of the census data, these data would be of greater use to the churches if the denominations are differentiated. While it would be possible to aggregate denominational groups for ecumenical purposes, important information would be lost if the denominational question were not asked in the first place. Such information should facilitate rather than impede realistic ecumenical cooperation.

Fourth, experience from the census test had already shown that some Christians are unwilling to use the general category 'Christian' and insisted on clarifying this category by writing in their denomination.

Fifth, it is likely that a significant application of the religious question within the census would be to amplify the ethnic question. In this context information about denominational affiliation may be of greater value than the global category of Christian.

Sixth, the censuses operated in Canada, New Zealand and Australia all find it beneficial to differentiate between Christian denominations. There may be advantages, it was argued, in international comparability.

The debate regarding the value of subdividing the Christian category had earlier been rehearsed in a symposium held on 3 July 1997 at the University of Southampton and reported in *Patterns of Prejudice* 32 (1998). In this context Barry Kosmin made four main points: that failure to subdivide the Christian category exposes other faith groups as small and marginal; that larger differences may exist within the Christian category than between faith groups; that the practical use of census data needs denominational differentiation; and that failure to follow the precedent adapted elsewhere frustrates international comparison both within Europe and within the Commonwealth.

These arguments were neither addressed nor heeded by the Office for National Statistics. The Census White Paper (1999) placed before parliament made the following proposal:

> 65. A decision to include the question in the 2001 Census in England and Wales depends on a change to the census legislation being made (see paragraph 176). The proposed question is:
>
> **What is your religion?**
> Tick one box only
> ☐ None
> ☐ Christian (including Church of England, Catholic, Protestant and all other Christian denominations)
> ☐ Buddhist
> ☐ Hindu
> ☐ Muslim
> ☐ Sikh
> ☐ Jewish
> ☐ Any other religion, *please write in below*
>
> ....

> 176. The proposal described at paragraphs 64–65 to include a question on religion in England and Wales in the 2001 Census would require a change to the primary legislation, since the Schedule to Census Act 1920 does not, as currently worded, permit such a question to be asked. Such an amendment would be necessary before a question on religion could be specified in the subsequent Order in Council for England and Wales. Before deciding whether to take such a step however, the government would want to be satisfied that the inclusion of such a question in a census commanded the necessary support of the general public.

The Scottish Parliament argued strenuously for the inclusion of Christian denominations and the question was changed accordingly. The Westminster Parliament accepted the Government's proposal as it stood.

An empirical test

Against this background, the aim of the present analysis is to test the extent to which different levels of social significance are generated by data which distinguish between the Christian denominations and data which collapse the different denominations into a single category styled 'Christian'. For such an analysis to be undertaken, two conditions need to be met. The first condition concerns the specification of an area in which religious affiliation may itself carry social significance. The second condition concerns the identification of a database which contains the appropriate markers both of religious affiliation and of social significance.

The area of social significance selected for analysis is that of social capital, as discussed, for example, in the pioneering work of Robert D. Putnam. The database capable of examining the relationships between religious affiliation and social capital is provided by the 1998 British Social Attitude Survey.[15] The hypothesis to be tested is that indicators of social capital are more strongly predicted from knowledge about denominational affiliation than from knowledge about being Christian in general.

Data from the British Social Attitudes Survey have already been employed by several commentators to address issues concerned with social capital. For example, Johnston and Jowell[16] interrogate these data to discuss 'social capital and the social fabric', and employ these data[17] to examine the question 'how robust is British civil society?' Data from the British Social Attitudes Survey have also been employed to examine the relationship between 'churchgoing and Christian ethics'.[18] As yet, however, these data have never been employed to examine the potential relationship between *religious affiliation* and *social capital*. The following analysis, therefore, sets out to do precisely this.

Social capital

The concept of social capital has become a popular analytic tool among academics, politicians and social commentators. Broadly defined, social capital is based on 'connections among individuals – social networks and the norms of reciprocity and trustworthiness that arise from them'.[19] In a similar analysis of the concept,[20] Hall argues that social capital is 'understood as the propensity of individuals to associate together on a regular basis, to trust one another, and to engage in community affairs'. Decline in social capital is often thought to be responsible for a damaging loss in social cohesion and mutual support. According to Rotberg[21] social capital works in the following manner.

Trust and reciprocity in human endeavour provide the basis for effective group action. A dearth of social capital in a society hinders social mobilization as well as political and economic growth. High levels of social capital, reflecting reciprocal bonds of trust, cut horizontally across classes and ethnicities and encourage cooperation and commonweal.

Putnam's analysis proceeds to distinguish between two forms of social capital. The first form is styled bonding social capital. This refers, for example, to the ways in which voluntary associational bodies display self interest by serving the needs of their own members. In this sense, the government may well be interested in the ways in which religious communities provide support for their own close adherents. Bonding social capital could be expressed informally through enhancing the psychological and social wellbeing of members through caring networks. Bonding social capital could be expressed more formally through activities like the provision of sheltered accommodation for ageing members. Such bonding social capital relieves certain pressures from the social services.

The second form is styled bridging social capital. This refers, for example, to ways in which voluntary associational bodies display altruism by serving the needs of the wider local community. In this sense, the government may well be interested in the ways in which religious communities provide support for the residents of their wider locality. Bridging social capital could be expressed informally through motivating members to serve on local committees, to undertake voluntary work and to be 'good neighbours' to all and sundry. Bridging social capital could be expressed more formally through operating day centres for the elderly, night shelters for the homeless, or employment schemes for the unemployed. Such bridging social capital relieves certain pressures from a wide range of government departments.

In a series of three recent papers,[22] Bruce, Gill and Davie have engaged in the debate regarding the extent to which decline in churchgoing may or may not reflect a wider decline in fondness for public association. The purpose of the present analysis is to test a very different thesis, namely the extent to which religious affiliation (not churchgoing) functions as a predictor of other indicators of social capital in contemporary England and Wales. Some recent studies conducted in the United States of America have already confirmed such a link between religion and community voluntarism[23] and voluntary association participation.[24]

British Social Attitudes Survey 1998

The main body of the British Social Attitudes Survey 1998 was conducted by interview among 3,146 individuals.[25] The interviews were supplemented by three versions of a self-completion questionnaire. Some questions were presented in all three versions, some in two versions, and some in one version only. Data from the self-completion questionnaires vary between 814 and 2,546 respondents, depending on which version or versions of the questionnaires contained the specific question.

Of the 3,146 individuals interviewed, 2,695 lived in England, 270 in Scotland, and 181 in Wales. Only the English data are employed in the present analysis. Of these 2,695 individuals, 37 provided no data on religious affiliation, 31 identified themselves as Muslim, 15 as Hindu, 10 as Jewish, 4 as Sikh, 2 as Buddhist, and 9 as belonging to other non-Christian groups. These 108 individuals were omitted from the subsequent analysis, which was consequently conducted among the remaining 2,587 respondents: 1,211 (47 per cent) individuals who claimed no religious affiliation and 1,376 (53 per cent) individuals who identified with Christianity. A large number of denominations were named by those who identified with the Christian tradition. The two largest groups were 815 Anglicans (32 per cent) and 243 Roman Catholics (9 per cent). Since no other group was large enough to sustain separate statistical analysis, the other 318 Christians (12 per cent) were grouped together. This is a clear weakness of the present analysis, but properly reflects the current difficulty of sustaining survey style research on the smaller religious groups in England today. For example, the next two largest denominational groups in the sample comprised 73 Methodists and 26 Baptists.

Looking at the individuals who described themselves as Christians, the data confirm both the way in which self-assigned religious affiliation functions as an indicator in its own right and not as a proxy for religious belief and religious practice, and the way in which the relationship between affiliation, belief, and practice vary from one denomination to another.[26] Thus, the classic Christian view that 'God concerns himself with humans' was endorsed by 35 per cent of the Anglicans, 57 per cent of the Roman Catholics, 65 per cent of the other Christians, and 12 per cent of those who owned no religious affiliation. Church attendance 'at least once in two weeks' was practised by 10 per cent of Anglicans, 38 per cent of Roman Catholics, 42 per cent of other Christians, and 1 per cent of those who owned no religious affiliation. Prayer 'nearly weekly' was practised by 37 per cent of Anglicans, 54 per cent of Roman Catholics, 64 per cent of other Christians, and 11 per cent of those who owned no religious affiliation.

Religious affiliation and social capital

In their analysis of social capital and the social fabric, based on the 1998 British Social Attitudes Survey data, Johnston and Jowell draw attention to three particular markers of social capital which sustain the social fabric of British society, in terms of faith in the democratic process, participation in community life, and civic engagement and social trust.

Regarding faith in the democratic process, Johnston and Jowell[27] argue that 'one symptom of a perceived deterioration in "citizenship" is declining turnout in elections'. They point to the poor turnout for the general election of 1997, followed by record low turnouts for local and European elections in 1998 and 1999. Although there is no way at present of measuring the relationship between attendance at the polling station and religious affiliation, there is every opportunity for the British Social Attitudes Survey to assess the relationship between religious affiliation and political attitudes, political intentions and self-reported previous political behaviours.

In response to the question, 'How much interest do you generally have in what is going on in politics?', 31 per cent of Anglicans, 31 per cent of Roman Catholics and 33 per cent of other Christians responded 'a great deal' or 'quite a lot', compared with 25 per cent of non-affiliates ($X^2 = 34.0$, $P < .001$). In response to a somewhat different question on political engagement, 50 per cent of Anglicans, 43 per cent of Roman Catholics, and 48 per cent of other Christians reported that they considered themselves to be a 'supporter of any one political party', compared with 34 per cent of non-affiliates ($X^2 = 56.3$, $P < .001$). Then in response to the question, 'If there was a general election tomorrow, which political party do you think you would be most likely to support?' only 7 per cent of Anglicans, 13 per cent of Roman Catholics, and 12 per cent of other Christians replied 'none', compared with 15 per cent of non-affiliates ($X^2 = 81.2$, $P < .001$).

So far knowledge about *Christian* affiliation seems to provide a significant predictor of political engagement. When the question is refined, however, into one concerned with support for specific political parties, *denominational* affiliation becomes so much more important. Support for the Conservative Party was provided by 39 per cent of Anglicans, 26 per cent of Roman Catholics, 27 per cent of other Christians and 24 per cent of non-affiliates. Support for the Labour Party was provided by 41 per cent of Anglicans, 53 per cent of Roman Catholics, 45 per cent of other Christians and 50 per cent of non-affiliates. Support for the Liberal Democratic Party was provided by 13 per cent of Anglicans, 8 per cent of Roman Catholics, 16 per cent of other Christians and 11 per cent of non-affiliates ($X^2 = 84.2$, $P < .001$). It is likely that rather different forms of social capital are associated with different political persuasions.

Regarding participation in community life, Johnston and Jowell[28] argue that 'Britain's rich community life has long been held up as an example of a strong social fabric ... A more important question, however, may be who participates in the activities of these organisations?' Their own analysis of the data, however, leaves this crucial question hanging.

A key question in the British Social Attitudes Survey asked, 'Are you currently a member of any of these groups: tenants or residents association, parent-teachers, school governors, political party, parish or town council, neighbourhood council, neighbourhood watch, local conservation or environmental group, other local community or voluntary group, or voluntary groups to help the sick, elderly, children, or other vulnerable people?' A positive answer to this question was given by 32 per cent of Christian affiliates and 21 per cent of non-affiliates. The single Christian category, however, disguises considerable variation between 34 per cent of Anglicans, 25 per cent of Roman Catholics, 33 per cent of other Christians and 21 per cent of non-affiliates ($X^2 = 48.8$, $P < .001$).

A similar kind of disparity is found among the Christian category in response to the focused question examining a more specialized minority interest. When asked, 'Are you a member of any kind of local cultural group such as an art or drama club?' once again the Roman Catholic profile was closer to the non-affiliates than to the Anglicans and to the other Christians. Membership of such cultural groups was affirmed by 7 per cent of Anglicans and 10 per cent of other Christians, compared with 6 per cent of Roman Catholics and 5 per cent of non-affiliates ($X^2 = 11.0$, $P < .01$).

A third question designed to tap another dimension of participation in community life focused on 'volunteer work'. Overall, volunteer work was undertaken 'at least once last year' by 27 per cent of Christians and 15 per cent of non-affiliates. Once again, however, the differences between the denominations are as large as the difference between the Christians and the non-affiliates. Volunteer work was undertaken at least once last year by 25 per cent of Anglicans, 27 per cent of Roman Catholics, 36 per cent of other Christians, and 15 per cent of non-affiliates ($X^2 = 34.4$, $P < .001$).

Regarding civic engagement and social trust, Johnston and Jowell[29] argue that 'one of the key putative components of social capital is the extent of trust that people have in others'. Then they cite a question posed by the British Social Attitudes Survey capable of testing the general level of trust in society.

> How often do you think that people would try to take advantage of you if they got the chance and how often would they try to be fair?

The view that people would try to be fair was taken by 64 per cent of the Christian affiliates and by 52 per cent of the non-affiliates. The differences between the denominations, however, are really considerable. On this issue the position taken by the Roman Catholics is the same as that taken by the non-affiliates. Thus, 52 per cent of Roman Catholics and 52 per cent of non-affiliates think that people would try to be fair, compared with 64 per cent of Anglicans and 77 per cent of other Christians (X^2 = 18.9, P < .01).

In order to examine how embedded people were within their communities, the British Social Attitudes Survey asked how comfortable people would be in asking their neighbours for help in various situations. One question posed the following scenario.

> Suppose that you were in bed ill and needed someone to go to the chemist to collect your prescription while they were doing their shopping. How comfortable would you be in asking a neighbour to do this?

At first glance there appeared to be only a slight difference between the levels of trust displayed by Christians or by non-affiliates, since the response 'very comfortable' or 'fairly comfortable' was given by 81 per cent of the Christians and by 77 per cent of the non-affiliates. Closer attention to denominational affiliation, however, showed religious affiliation to be a significant predictor. While 77 per cent of non-affiliates, 77 per cent of Roman Catholics and 76 per cent of other Christians were 'very comfortable' or 'fairly comfortable' in asking for this kind of help, the proportion rose to 85 per cent among Anglicans (X^2 = 13.8, P < .01).

Conclusion

On the basis of their original analysis, Johnston and Jowell[30] concluded that 'Britain still contains many elements of a strong civil society with extensive opportunities for the accumulation of social capital'. They also drew attention to the way in which two social markers routinely gathered by the census predicted significant variations in levels of social capital, namely age and class. According to their analysis, social capital was lower among 'young people' and among 'the poorer sections of society'. The present analysis has extended Johnston and Jowell's original conclusions in two ways.

First, attention has been drawn to the significance of the question on religious affiliation as a third significant predictor of variations in levels of social capital. Even the relatively crude measure of religious affiliation provided in the 2001 census for England and Wales will be able to predict some variations in levels of social capital across the country. Moreover, if affiliation to the Christian tradition is in decline, as suggested by many commentators,[31] the government might well be wise to anticipate some consequent erosion in social capital.

Second, however, attention has also been drawn to the way in which a census question which fails to distinguish between different Christian denominations may provide information which is not only inadequate but also possibly misleading. The advice offered by the Office for National Statistics not to subdivide the Christian category seems to have been wrongly accepted by the Westminster Parliament, and a better informed position seems to have been adopted by the Scottish Parliament. Sufficient informed debate is now needed to correct the situation in time for the 2011 census in England and Wales.

What the present analysis has now tested and established regarding the relationship between self-assigned denominational affiliation and social capital needs to be replicated by further analyses concerned with the relationship between self-assigned denominational affiliation and other issues of social significance.

NOTES

1. The research project underpinning the present chapter has been supported by a grant from the Arts and Humanities Research Board. I am grateful to Dr Michael Fearn for his support with this project.
2. See Great Britain, Census Office, *Census of Great Britain 1851: Religious Worship in England and Wales*; Jones, I. G. and Williams, D. (eds), *The Religious Census of 1851 ... (South Wales)*; and Jones, I. G., *The Religious Census of 1851 ... (North Wales)*.
3. Jowell, R. and others, *British Social Attitudes: the 16th Report*, p. 363.
4. Francis, L. J. and Astley, J., *Psychological Perspectives on Prayer*.
5. Kaldor, P. and others, *Taking Stock*.
6. See Jowell and others, *British Social Attitudes: the 16th Report*, p. 329.
7. Jowell and others, *British Social Attitudes: the 16th Report*, p. 328.
8. Statistics New Zealand, *2001 Census of Population and Dwellings*, p. 112.
9. See Francis, L. J., *Youth in Transit*.
10. Bouma, G. D., *Religion*, pp. 106–7.
11. Bouma, *Religion*, p. 108, emphasis added.
12. See Zavalloni, M., 'Social identity and the recording of reality', p. 200.
13. Wallis, R. and Bruce, S., 'Secularization: the orthodox model'.
14. Internal document prepared for the Office for National Statistics.
15. See Jowell and others, *British Social Attitudes: the 16th Report*.
16. Johnston, M. and Jowell, R., 'Social capital and the social fabric'.
17. Johnston, M. and Jowell, R., 'How robust is British civil society?'
18. Gill, R., *Churchgoing and Christian Ethics*.
19. Putnam, R. D., *Bowling Alone*, p. 19.
20. Hall, P. A., 'Social capital in Britain', p. 417.

21. Rotberg, R. I., 'Social capital and political culture', p. 2.
22. Bruce, S., 'Praying alone?'; Gill, R., 'A response to Steve Bruce's "Praying alone?"'; Davie, G., 'Praying alone?'
23. Park, J. Z. and Smith, C., 'To whom much has been given...'
24. Lam, P.-Y., 'As the flocks gather'.
25. I am grateful to the British Social Attitudes Survey and to the United Kingdom Data Archive for the use of these data and acknowledge the following source: *Social and Community Planning Research, British Social Attitudes Survey, 1998* [computer file]. Colchester: UK Data Archive [distributor], 8 June 2000. SN: 4131.
26. In accordance with instructions issued by the National Centre for Social Research, *1998 British Spocial Attitudes Survey: Note for Users*, the data are weighted in all subsequent analyses. Households were selected randomly during the BSA survey with equal probability. However, only one person in each household was interviewed. People in small households, therefore, have a higher probability of being selected than people in large households. The weighting variable corrects for this.
27. Johnston and Jowell, 'Social capital and the social fabric', p. 179.
28. 'Social capital and the social fabric', pp. 181–2.
29. 'Social capital and the social fabric', p. 186.
30. 'Social capital and the social fabric', p. 193.
31. Brierley, P., *'Christian' England*; Bruce, 'Praying alone?'

REFERENCES AND FURTHER READING

Berger, P., *The Sacred Canopy: Elements of a Sociology of Religion*. New York, Doubleday, 1967.

Berger, P., *A Rumour of Angels: Modern Society and the Rediscovery of the Supernatural*. Harmondsworth, Penguin Books, 1971.

Bibby, R. W., 'Religious encasement in Canada: an argument for Protestant and Catholic entrenchment' in *Social Compass* 16 (1985), pp. 287–303.

Bibby, R. W., *Fragmented Gods: the Poverty and Potential of Religion in Canada*. Toronto, Irwin Publishing, 1987.

Bouma, G. D., *Religion: Meaning, Transcendence and Community in Australia*. Melbourne, Longman Cheshire, 1992.

Brierley, P., *'Christian' England*. London, MARC Europe, 1991.

Bruce, S., *God is Dead: Secularisation in the West*. Oxford, Blackwell, 2002.

Bruce, S., 'Praying alone? Churchgoing in Britain and the Putnam thesis' in *Journal of Contemporary Religion* 17 (2002), pp. 317–28.

Davie, G., *Religion in Britain since 1945: Believing without Belonging*. Oxford, Blackwell, 1994.

Davie, G., 'Praying alone? Churchgoing in Britain and social capital: a reply to Steve Bruce' in *Journal of Contemporary Religion* 17 (2002), pp. 329–34.

Fane, R. S., 'Is self-assigned religious affiliation socially significant?' in Francis, L. J. (ed.), *Sociology, Theology and the Curriculum* (London, Cassell, 1999), pp 113–24.

Francis, L. J., *Youth in Transit: a Profile of 16–25 year olds*. Aldershot, Gower, 1982.

Francis, L. J. and Astley, J., *Psychological Perspectives on Prayer: a Reader*. Leominster, Gracewing, 2001.

Gill, R., *Churchgoing and Christian Ethics*. Cambridge, Cambridge University Press, 1999.

Gill, R., 'A response to Steve Bruce's "Praying Alone?" ' in *Journal of Contemporary Religion* 17 (2002), pp. 335–8.

Great Britain, Census Office, *Census of Great Britain 1851: Religious Worship in England and Wales – Abridged from the Official Report made by Horace Mann to George Graham Esq Registrar General*. London, Routledge, 1854.

Great Britain, Treasury, *The 2001 Census of Population* (Cm. 4253). London, The Stationery Office, 1999.

Hall, P. A., 'Social capital in Britain' in *British Journal of Political Science* 29 (1999), pp. 417–61.

Johnston, M. and Jowell, R., 'Social capital and the social fabric' in Jowell, R., Curtice, J., Park, A. and Thomson, K. (eds), *British Social Attitudes: the 16th report* (Aldershot, Ashgate, 1999), pp. 179–200.

Johnston, M. and Jowell, R., 'How robust is British civil society?' in Park, A., Curtice, J., Thomson, K., Jarvis, L. and Bromley, C. (eds), *British Social Attitudes: the 18th report* (London, Sage, 2001), pp. 175–97.

Jones, I. G. (ed.), *The Religious Census of 1851: a Calendar of the Returns Relating to Wales (North Wales)*. Cardiff, University of Wales Press, 1981.

Jones, I. G. and Williams, D. (eds), *The Religious Census of 1851: a Calendar of the Returns Relating to Wales (Volume 1, South Wales)*. Cardiff, University of Wales Press, 1976.

Jowell, R., Curtice, J., Park, A. and Thomson, K., *British Social Attitudes: the 16th Report*. Aldershot, Ashgate, 1999.

Kaldor, P., Dixon, R. and Powell, R., *Taking Stock: a profile of Australian Church Attenders*, Adelaide, South Australia, Openbook Publishers, 1999.

Kosmin, B. A., 'A religious question in the British census' in *Patterns of Prejudice* 32:2 (1998), pp. 39–46.

Lam, P.-Y., 'As the flocks gather: how religion affects voluntary association participation' in *Journal for the Scientific Study of Religion* 41 (2002), pp. 405–22.

National Centre for Social Research, *1998 British Social Attitudes Survey: Note for Users*. London, National Centre for Social Research, 2000.

Park, J. Z. and Smith, C., 'To whom much has been given . . .': religious capital and community voluntarism among churchgoing Protestants' in *Journal for the Scientific Study of Religion* 39 (2000), pp. 272–86.

Putnam, R. D., *Bowling Alone: the Collapse and Revival of American Community*. New York, Touchstone, 2000.

Rotberg, R. I., 'Social capital and political culture in Africa, America, Australasia, and Europe' in Rotberg, R. I. (ed.), *Patterns of Social Capital: stability and change in historical perspectives* (Cambridge, Cambridge University Press, 2001), pp. 1–17.

Statistics New Zealand, *2001 Census of Population and Dwellings: Preliminary Views on Content*. Wellington, Statistics New Zealand, 1998.

Wallis, R. and Bruce, S., 'Secularization: the orthodox model' in Bruce, S. (ed.), *Religion and Modernization: Sociologists and Historians Debate the Secularisation Thesis*. (Oxford, Clarendon Press, 1992), pp. 8–30.

Zavalloni, M., 'Social identity and the recording of reality: its relevance for cross-cultural psychology' in *International Journal of Psychology* 10 (1975), pp. 197–217.

5

Addressing Complexity: A Psychosocial Approach to Thinking about Religion

Wesley Carr

Introduction

As I am redrafting this paper, the media are marking the fifth anniversary of the death and funeral of Princess Diana. Even after five years, some of the phenomena remain powerful. Why did people queue for hours into the night and early morning to write in the books of condolence? Why did so many turn up so early for the funeral? Why were the people in the crowds so courteous to one another and quiet in the Mall and St James's? Why were people so pleased when the Union Jack flew at half mast over Buckingham Palace? What role(s) did Her Majesty the Queen play in her address to the nation? The questions about human behaviour are endless. They will bear partial interpretation in psychological or sociological terms. But there is always a third dimension to include – the theological basis on which the church (in this instance Westminster Abbey) ministers on such an occasion.

The contemporary social sciences in all their variety and richness have much to contribute to understanding religious belief and the church's engagement with people and their beliefs. But, although it is a generalization, most clergy find sociological approaches and psychological stances less helpful than they might hope. For they seem to present a choice of ways of looking rather than a unifying and clarifying approach to the church's work. In addition, they methodologically exclude theology. Each is an academic discipline in its own right, but not necessarily of direct help to someone trying to make sense of the church and of people's beliefs and the engagement between the two. What is more, working ministers face decisions and action, but sociological or psychological studies appear reductionist.[1] Robert Browning captured that feeling in *Bishop Blougram's Apology* (1855):

> How you'd exult if I could put you back
> Six hundred years, blot out cosmogony,
> Geology, ethnology, what not
> (Greek endings, each the little passing-bell
> That signifies some faith's about to die),
> And set you square with Genesis again...

Holding disciplines together

We need a way of holding together the complexities of even the most simple occasion, as modern human sciences increasingly expose them, and the theological dimension that is uniquely the church's. The psychodynamic approach offers such a possibility, for it is concerned with understanding leading to action and not learning for its own sake.

In the United Kingdom this stance, also known as 'systems psychodynamics', 'the socio-technical approach' or 'action research', is primarily associated with the Tavistock Institute.[2] While the sort of data collected in sociological and psychological studies is used, the method is concerned with interchange and with making the institution more effective.

> Action research was to be central to the Tavistock Institute's mission: to advance social science through involvement in practical human problems and concerns. And action research, by its nature, is problem-centred, not discipline-centred.[3]

Interaction and interpretation

The approach is marked by interaction and interpretation of what is happening here and now. Therefore the fact of writing itself freezes a 'here-and-now' and thus takes away its immediacy. The approach has three main components: research, consultancy and experiential learning. The seminal book remains that by Eric J. Miller and A. Kenneth Rice, *Systems of Organization* (1967). The authors attempt to integrate ideas and theories which were emerging from three fields: systems theory, the study of group relations and psychoanalysis. The group relations study is the laboratory where systems and psychodynamics are exposed. Psychodynamics refers to the psychoanalytic approach to the significance of experience and mental processes both in the individual and in the group. The theoretical basis of this lies largely in the work of Melanie Klein with her emphasis on the persistence of primitive anxieties and the way in which we construct defences against them. The significance of social defences, therefore, is one of the earliest understandings of this approach and one of its seminal ideas. Menzies, in a classic paper,[4] drew attention to the way in which personal and group feeling and belief may hinder or assist work at the organization's task.[5]

Through this action-related theory a crucial link is opened up for scrutiny, namely that between the individual and the group. This is an essential nexus for anyone working with people, especially in such an organization as a church. There are always two facets – the individual and the group. For example, there is the believer with his or her own psychological expectations and the congregation or some other group with an agenda. Anyone working in such a context knows that these two dimensions have both to be held. The difficulty is finding a way of addressing them together, for 'the individual is the creature of the group, the group of the individual'.[6] This primary link has recently been hypothesized as extending to the connections and connectedness[7] between the individual and society.[8]

There remains the systems aspect. Open systems theory derives from biology.[9] It posits that, like a living organism, an effective organization 'lives' by a process of input, transformation and output.[10] The combination of these two basic stances – the psychoanalytical approach applied through the group to larger entities, coupled with systems theory, creates the psychodynamic or socio-technical approach. It is marked by attention to both conscious (system) and unconscious (analytical) behaviour, to issues of covert process and especially in the exercise of authority, work task and activities. In other words, it goes to the core of the church's activity. Action research, for instance, is not concerned with 'ministry' but with 'ministers'.

Studying groups and society

Wilfred Bion, whose *Experiences in Groups* (1961) is a seminal (though not easy) text, discovered that a group's behaviour could be studied and interpreted in itself. Like individuals, groups had their own unconscious life. Two levels of functioning could be discerned: 'work' and 'basic assumption'.

Any group of people is marked by basic assumption or unconscious behaviour: dependence, fight/flight and pairing.[11] The dependent group seeks someone (often the consultant – or, of course, minister or priest) who is reckoned to have some authority and on whom to rely so that they themselves do not have to become responsible. Pairing is an intensified form of this, when a pair is set up to produce a new leader, who is then often killed off. And fight/flight, which are two aspects of the same dynamic, describes a group that is dissociating from its task. Bion contrasted the group's basic assumptions, its unconscious behaviour, with its work, the reason for its being there in the first place.

But he took this hypothesis a stage further – one which proved important for thinking about the church and its mission. He suggested that the three basic assumptions were also dealt with in society by certain institutions. For example, the church holds dependence. It is used to reassure people about the ultimate aspect of life, to manage the last great unknown, death. It can do so because it is believed to be in touch with the ultimate reliable object – God. By contrast, the military represent fight. We can put the two together. The services are keen to keep padres (clergy) because the soldier, sailor or airman puts his life on the line and can do so more confidently if he knows that, if he is killed, his death will be noted and marked by the church. One consequence is that the services did not want Non Stipendiary Ministrers.[12] When in a foxhole you have to be quite clear whether your companion is a padre to bury you or a soldier to kill with you. The soldier carries the fight on behalf of the non-fighting dimension; the church, which takes on dependence for the soldiers, holds this.[13]

The life of any organization, therefore, can be differentiated into two parts: the task group, which is the collection of individuals who constitute the organization in its activity, and the sentient group, who are the same people considered in terms of their commitment and of their reliance on the group for emotional support.

Dependence and the distinctive task of churches

Within this general theory churches present interesting questions. For Miller and Rice

> A church is characterised by its members' collective belief in a deity or system of deities on whom they can depend. Belief in a deity involves belief in some kind of life after death. The sentient system of a church . . . is unbounded, in that it has no ending. In the spiritual sense there is no export system.[14]

That understanding assumes that churches are closed systems and precludes the socio-technical approach. However, churches have proved amenable to such study. Richard Herrick, Canon of Chelmsford Cathedral, and Bruce Reed of Christian Teamwork, later the Grubb Institute, attended the first conference.[15] With others they reflected further on dependence. They realized that churches (and in England especially the Church of England) do indeed handle the dependent aspects of people's lives. Reed refined the idea with such terms as 'extra-dependence' and 'intra dependence' (later terms included 'mature' and 'immature') to describe the two main states of dependence. Immature dependence is the equivalent of Bion's basic assumption; mature dependence is found when it is harnessed to the task in hand. Reed and his colleagues showed that the church takes immature dependence (that is, people's abandoning of themselves to some other without reflection) and puts it through a transformative process and exports people in a more mature state of dependence (responsible joining with God).[16] This process can be discerned not only in the life of a local church; it also marks national life. The funeral of Princess Diana was a particularly rich example of this process at societal as well as individual levels.

The use of counter-transference

The strength of the psycho-social approach to the topic of religion and faith is that it makes no pretence to dispassionate objectivity. It is action research and the interchange between the researcher and the body being studied itself indicates issues to be addressed. The work of the scholar or consultant in a particular field involves him or her specifically not as a passive (or even less objective) observer but as integral to the process. But for such working a grasp of counter-transference is essential. Whatever the overall assessment of Freud's theories, the discovery of transference is fundamental. It was first a clinical symptom, but was soon recognized as part of everyday life; counter-transference was not so much studied. But it has increasingly become a key concept in action research: 'the consultant's feelings may provide significant evidence about the underlying feelings with the client system'.[17]

An example of how this works may be seen in a consultation to a psychiatric unit.

> Prior to the consultation it was possible to assume that transference and counter-transference were technical issues that concerned therapists and patients alone and that stresses and tensions between hospital subgroups represented either personality issues or traditional behavior: 'Doctors always devalue nurses.' Yet when the shared treatment task was defined and the institution examined as a whole, it became apparent that those unbearable feelings in the staff which revealed centrally important and interpretable aspects of patients' treatment could be exposed by examining all the relationships within the unit ... Each interaction represented more disguised transference and countertransference than the participants realised.[18]

It will by now be clear that this approach is undergirded with theory but at the same time is intensely practical.[19] It is a familiar complaint that sociological and psychological studies complicate work that is already difficult enough. By contrast the socio-technical approach can be used with any form of institution and is a key to exploration at a range of levels because it pays attention to human behaviour in any context.[20] It also addresses underlying processes and what they represent. And issues of authority and leadership are rarely absent, although they are beyond the capacity of the client to perceive without consultancy.[21]

The consequences of the socio-technical approach

This approach uniquely links irrational and rational processes within both individual and group, which may range from our first organization (the family) to vast concepts such as society. It offers a means of holding together those insights into the individual and society alike which have been generated by the behavioural sciences during the twentieth century. In what follows I refer to clergy or ministers, but the same basic stance applies in studying church organization. Because the underlying problem in many instances turns out to be one of authority, the public role of the minister is likely to receive more attention than it is given in contemporary theologies of the church and ordained ministry. In his or her formal role the minister is required to hold together both the individual and the social context of ministry. Here the realities of belief and the developing theologies encounter each other and can conflict. I have, for example, rarely met anyone, lay or ordained who instinctively feels meaning in the idea that at the eucharist the congregation is the celebrant and the priest the president. The dynamic richness of every context is affirmed and the minister cannot oversimplify the encounter.

Since there is no individual apart from a context, then in practice a large perspective is essential. There are two basic reasons. First, however intimate a meeting may appear (for example, a formal act of confession), it is always more than that. Behind each action there lies further reality: the range of unconscious assumptions is beyond imagining. Which fragment of such complexity is chosen for engagement is a matter of experience and judgement and this is where counter-transference is involved. Second, the issue of theology becomes prominent and unavoidable, since the approach demands of ministers the use of their distinctive perspective. It does not add another discipline, but points to the theological basis of ministry. For the other individual or group the minister represents the context of his or her belief, that is God and the Church.

The approach brings together aspects of human life which are integral to the minister's activity but which often feel disparate. For example, ministers might consider how they are to connect individual belief and idiosyncrasy with the corporate expression of faith in the Church. The question is endemic to Christianity and cannot be finally answered. But the minister has continually to address it.

> How do we evaluate claimed faith and belief in relation to psychological tendencies or even types? Is there a connection between feelings and faith? And what psychological or sociological function do we assign to belief? These are both major questions for the theologian and day-to-day material for the pastor. And what about the notion of 'the Church'? What is the connection between the organization which is necessary to produce an institution and the Christian imperative to freedom? Ministers, for example, may only be allowed to do their work in so far as they let themselves be seen as representatives of a institution – the Church. Yet often they will wish as a pastoral stratagem, or even in response to their own experience of pastoral ministry, to distance themselves from that church.[22]

Critique

The main risk with this stance is, as must now be obvious, being caught up in the dynamic in such a way that the person thinking about the Church and the world cannot disentangle him or herself from it. It is easy to poke holes in this way of approaching issues of religion, belief and the church. It is blatantly and unashamedly subjective. The question for anyone studying any aspect of religion in this way is: 'What is happening to me? And why?' But just as the consultant (or minister or priest) reaches this point and offers an interpretation, the fact of his or her so doing changes the dynamic and the search resumes. For such living, therefore, the prerequisite is flexibility and being able to live with and by hypotheses.

A second important factor is the supervision or consultancy to the person or institution. By maintaining contact outside the immediate situation, the minister or researcher can sustain some sense of himself or herself in relation to what is going on without collusion with the client. It is also essential that those working in this field have some understanding, both experiential and intellectual, of their counter-transference. Experiential learning is essential. To have to explain to another what you remember and think you have done in a consultation or encounter is a rigorous test of attention and understanding. It minimizes the room for collusion and associated errors. This approach is personal. It should, therefore, be likely both to assist someone better to understand their authority and to attempt to extrapolate from the fragments of an everyday encounter into a larger interpretation. In terms of contemporary church and religious life, the emphasis falls again on authority and dependence.

And what of grandiosity? The enthusiasm for an all-encompassing hypothesis or interpretation encourages the explorer always to press the interpretation a step further. There then occasionally emerges an unbelievable globalism which is no help to anyone. The difference between action research and casual coffee conversation is considerable. Our current social context seems to be one in which any exercise of authority with its associated moral issues is vulnerable. If no authority is acknowledged, then task related religious activity is rare. Dependence will almost always be the prevailing dynamic around churches. A grasp of that and an examination of authority together often leads to development. And the question of spirituality, vogue (and vague) word that it is, is both more prominent and difficult to handle, largely because we do not quite know what it is – it seems everything and nothing.

To estimate people's enthusiasm for spiritual matters is difficult. It seems (and I say this with hesitation) that we may have passed through a period when people could only move one way in relation to the church, and that was away from it. Some are finding ways back. But there is always a danger that church people will rush towards anything that sounds superficially encouraging. Grace Davie's book, *Religion in Britain since 1945,* provided the twin themes of believing and belonging. It is a phenomenon that demands attention, not least for its emphasis on the affective side to such hidden belief. But it was soon turned into a defensive slogan.

But if it is difficult to establish accurately the state of belief and practice, we may be sure that we are dealing with areas in the human being that have often been either ignored or explained away. This part of the self may be irreducible by analysis[23] and that therefore needs careful examination.[24] In this mode of behaviour, people are living between illusion and delusion. To survive they need a holding environment[25] to give them security to address the issue. Churches serve this purpose. Therapy diagnoses and treats extreme instances of trouble. Ministry functions in the same fashion, but not by diagnosing. It stands for transcendence and hope, the one being about God and the other being about belonging.

However, there is something uncomfortable happening; John Pridmore, Rector of Hackney, recently put it well:

> The spiritually hungry, who have no appetite for religion, now have stronger meat than wacky New Age spiritualities to sustain them. Robust models of spirituality are emerging which are socially attuned, imaginatively engaging and morally exacting, but which neither invoke

religious truth claims or nor require the application of strange-smelling substances to your person. The shaping of such spiritualities is being driven by educational legislation requiring that schools attend to the spiritual well-being of young people, irrespective of what provision is made for their religious education. There is little sign that the churches have yet woken up to the fact that this is happening.[26]

Such important primary data (he drew it from a conference on children's spirituality) will only be given attention by those trying to think about the Church if it is not categorized by one or other discipline. It needs simply to be taken as data, together with other reports of experience and made the stuff not of a policy but of an hypothesis. From the testing of this, further learning will arise. At present the Church of England (indeed all churches) seems to have no means of doing this. Its departmental officers (some very able) are tied into bureaucratic systems which prevent them from making thinking their daily work.

But what if this approach led to some hypotheses? What might they be? It is impossible, of course, to know. But the sort of areas I would expect to come under swift scrutiny might be the consequences for authority in the church of the proliferation of bishops. The dispersal of episcopal authority in this way may be an unconscious response to the centripetal tendencies of the departments and not least the diocesan bishops. The way in which people today expect to be personally known (e.g. by forename) and not encountered in role (e.g. Churchwarden, Treasurer) must be having an impact on all activity. In similar vein, why is it that the Church of England is unable to remove a tier of its central organization when everything else is being stripped down? The Archbishops' Council has not reduced the number of meetings of the General Synod; the synod did not lead to the expected disbandment of convocations. And how has the Church managed to shift the Church Commissioners into paying pensions when the money was originally taken for the Church's living activity? What is the impact of such decisions on the working church and ministerial integrity? When a stipend becomes a salary there may be more impact on faith and spirituality than is immediately apparent. These are the sort of issue that calls for examination as more than a matter of managerial decisions.

Conclusion

It would be naive to suggest that the theory of the individual, the group, society, basic assumptions and work groups and its elaboration magically solves problems. It would also be nonsense. Yet ministers and their colleagues in congregations, as well as those responsible for wider diocesan and national policies, need a working framework by which to hold together the disparate aspects of their activity. They are currently too bound by documents alone. The socio-technical approach is a useful counter to that. In particular it draws attention to the way that every person lives within a set of human institutions which can be thought of in a systemic fashion.

A church, whatever its particular denominational shape, can be conceived as a system in a state of some sort of dynamic disequilibrium. It represents a stance that seeks to encompass the complexities of role, person and context in a unique and for many a clarifying fashion. It may, of course, be that the church (at least the Church of England) is rolling steadily down towards its demise. That impression is given when figures are added up and compared. However, as is often commented, the figures 'feel' wrong: there seems to be much more interchange than the numbers suggest. One diocese recently carried out a study of the number of significant encounters between the clergy and people (anyone, not the congregation alone) in the course of a year. It found that an extraordinary percentage of people had such contact, not to mention any encounters with lay people that they knew. The Church and what it stands for is more deeply embedded in people's lives than we realize. What to do about it is a big question. But it is just the topic that action research or the psycho-social approach to organizations can best study.

NOTES

1. There are exceptions, e.g. Grace Davie *Religion in Britain since 1945* and Watts, Nye and Savage *Psychology for Christian Ministry*.
2. Church people are most likely to know of the Institute through the study of group relations. At one time this was widely incorporated into education programmes for clergy and laity, not least those run by the Church of England Board of Education.
3. Miller, E. J., *From Dependency to Autonomy*, pp. 7–8.
4. Menzies, I. E. P. (1967) is a classic example of such study.
5. Miller (*From Dependency to Autonomy*, p. 249) points out that 'published material is disappointingly scarce' and refers to E. Jacques 'Social systems as a defence against persecutory and depressive anxiety', on which Menzies drew. It should be noted that Jaques later abandoned this position (Jaques, 'Why the psychoanalytical approach to understanding organizations is dysfunctional').
6. Miller, E. J. and Rice, A. K., *Systems of Organization*, p. 17.
7. The distinction between these two terms parallels that drawn between 'relationship' and 'relatedness'. The first refers to personal encounter; the

second to the link between the individual or sub-group to the rest of its environment without any necessarily personal contact.

8. Khaleelee, O. and Miller, E. J., pp. 353–83.
9. Bertalanffy, L. von, *General system theory*.
10. It was an early point of dispute as to whether a church could be thought of as an open system. If the output was life after death, how could this be examined? See below, p. 69.
11. Two other basic assumptions have been proposed since Bion wrote, but neither has commanded the widespread acceptance of Bion's three.
12. Non Stipendiary Ministers are trained and ordained but do not leave their secular life and employment. They are therefore hybrid in conventional terms – both priest and lay – but sometimes not quite priestly enough (standing apart from 'professional' clergy, whether by their choice or the demands of the system) and no longer technically lay within the church but clearly so in their daily lives at work. This ambiguity is found throughout the Church.
13. The Church is not alone in this: similar issues arise with medical treatment of casualties.
14. Miller and Rice, *Systems of Organization*, p. 255.
15. Rice, A. K., *Learning for Leadership*.
16. Reed, B. D., *The Dynamics of Religion*.
17. Miller, *From Dependency to Autonomy*, p. 7.
18. Shapiro, E. R. and Carr, A. W., 'Disguised counter-transference', p. 118.
19. I was once told by a fellow dean that the secret of a happy cathedral was a successful annual pantomime.
20. Miller's collection of pieces (*From Dependence to Autonomy*) includes studies of government and water agencies, integrated development and the role of a diplomatic wife; among his clients have been an airline, residential institutions for incurables, geriatric hospitals, a diocese, a prison and a steelworks.
21. In an early work, *The Priestlike Task*, I suggested a consultancy model of ministry. The term did not catch on (in retrospect not surprisingly), although some have explored the ideas in their ministry.
22. Carr, A. W., *Handbook of Pastoral Studies*, p. 159.
23. See the titles by Rizzuto and Symington listed under References and Further Reading.
24. Carr, *Handbook of Pastoral Studies*, pp. 249ff. These are risky words. At the time of the funeral of Princess Diana, I made a comment on these lines and some journalists, without enquiring, reported that I was calling people mad.
25. Winnicott, D.W., *Through Pediatrics to Psychoanalysis*.
26. *Church Times* (6 September 2002), p. 13.

REFERENCES AND FURTHER READING

Bertalanffy, L. von, *General System Theory*. Harmondsworth, Penguin, 1973.
Carr, A. W., *The Priestlike Task*. London, SPCK, 1985.
Carr, A. W., 'Postscript: After the Miller/Lawrence Working Note (1991)' in Miller,

E. J., *From Dependency to Autonomy: Studies in Organization and Change* London, Free Association Books, 1993, pp. 117–20.

Carr, A. W., 'Some consequences of conceiving society as a large group' in *Group: The Journal of the Eastern Group Psychotherapy Society* 17 (1993), pp. 235–44.

Carr, A. W., *Handbook of Pastoral Studies,* London, SPCK, 1997.

Carr, A. W., 'Irrationality and Religion', reprinted in Carr, *Handbook of Pastoral Studies,* Appendix 3, pp. 249–65.

Carr, A. W., 'The Exercise of Authority in a Dependent Context' in Gould et al., pp. 45–66.

Davie, G., *Religion in Britain since 1945: Believing without Belonging.* Oxford, Blackwell, 1994.

Gould, L., 'Introduction' in Gould, L. J., Stapley, L. F., and Stein, M., *The Systems Psychodynamics of Organizations: Integrating the Group Relations Approach, Psychoanalytic and Open Systems Perspectives: Contributions in Honor of Eric J. Miller.* London and New York, Karnac Press, 2001.

Jaques, E., 'Social systems as a defence against persecutory and depressive anxiety' in Klein, M., Heimann, P. and Money-Kyrle, R. E. (eds), *New Directions in Psycho-Analysis* (London, Tavistock, 1955), pp. 478–98.

Jaques, E., 'Social systems as a defence against anxiety' in Lyth, I. Menzies, *Containing Anxiety in Institutions: Selected Essays 1* (London, Free Association Press, 1989), pp. 43–85.

Jaques, E., 'Why the psychoanalytical approach to understanding organizations is dysfunctional', *Human Relations* 48 (1995), pp. 343–65.

Khaleelee, O. and Miller, E. J., 'Beyond the small group: society as an intelligible field for study' in Pines (1985), pp. 353–83.

Klein, M., *Our Adult World and Other Essays,* Heinemann, London, 1963.

McCutcheon, R. T., *The Insider/Outsider Problem in the Study of Religion: A Reader.* Cassell, London and New York, 1999.

Menzies, I. E. P., 'A case study in the functioning of social systems as a defence against anxiety', in A. D. Colman and W. H. Bexton (eds), *Group Relations Reader 1.* Washington DC, 1967. (Often reprinted in various collections.)

Miller, E. J., *From Dependency to Autonomy: Studies in Organization and Change.* London, Free Association Press, 1993.

Miller, E. J., 'The politics of involvement' in *Journal of Personality and Social Systems* (1980), pp. 37–50.

Miller, E. J. and Rice, A. K., *Systems of Organization: The Control of Task and Sentient Boundaries.* London, Tavistock Publications, 1967.

Obholzer, A. and Roberts, V. Z. (eds), *The Unconscious at Work: Individual and Organizational Stress in the Human Services.* London, Routledge and Kegan Paul, 1994.

Pines, M. (ed.), *Bion and Group Psychotherapy.* London, Routledge and Kegan Paul, 1985.

Reed, B. D., *The Dynamics of Religion: Process and Movement in Christian Churches.* London, Darton, Longman and Todd, 1978.

Rice, A. K., *Learning for Leadership.* London, Tavistock, 1966.

Rizzuto, A.-M., *The Birth of the Living God*. Chicago, Chicago University Press, 1979.

Shapiro, E. R. and Carr, A. W., 'Disguised counter-transference in institutions' in *Psychiatry* 50 (1987), pp. 72–82.

Shapiro, E. R. and Carr, A. W., *Lost in Familiar Places: Making New Connections between the Individual and Society*. London and New Haven, Yale University Press, 1991.

Symington, N., *Emotion and Spirit: Questioning the Claims of Psychoanalysis and Religion*. London, Cassell, 1994.

Watts, F., Nye, R. and Savage, S., *Psychology for Christian Ministry*. London and New York, Routledge, 2002.

Winnicott, D. W., *Through Pediatrics to Psychoanalysis*. New York, Basic Books, 1951.

6

Interpreting Contemporary Spirituality

Anne Richards

One of the major missiological and apologetic tasks of the Christian Church today is that of offering the gospel as a viable, reasonable and living faith which is capable of turning around and transforming lives for ever. One reason why this is such a challenging task is that the people we meet are not simply empty vessels waiting to be filled with the Good News of Jesus Christ. Many of those who encounter the witness of the Church already have powerful beliefs and practices through which they express their encounters with, and their longing for, God. Some believe they walk with Christ, who blesses their endeavours, albeit outside the Church. Yet others have stories to tell of God at work in their lives in language unfamiliar to our accepted modes of Christian testimony. How do we make sense of such contemporary spirituality and what is the proper Christian response to it in the process of witnessing to others? This is an important challenge, because failure to respond to the spirituality of people outside the Church can lead to misunderstanding, breakdown in communication, and can make the mission possibilities of pastoral opportunities redundant. Conversely, should Christians 'buy into' people's spirituality, accepting its expression uncritically, especially when such spirituality may come with hostile perceptions of Church?

A personal spirituality

What then are the characteristics of contemporary spirituality outside the Church? First, it is often both personal and particular. For example:

A successful businesswoman bought a house with a large garden and spent a great deal of money on transforming the garden into a personal haven in which to spend her leisure time. The central area of the garden was paved, with seating that had come from a disused church. Within the paved area was a water feature, with a small fountain bubbling over stones set in an old stone basin which had also come from the church. With its scented flowers and herbs, this area of the garden became what the businesswoman described as her 'spiritual centre', the place where she felt close to God and where she could find peace after a busy day. She felt her relationship with some 'higher power' was expressed by the choice of water, wood and stone and by the particular combination of plants and herbs offering a play of colour, texture and scent.

What is interesting about this story is that it shows clearly some of the characteristics of 'spirituality' in our contemporary society. Such a 'spirituality' is part of our leisure activity; it is what we devote time to when we are not earning our money. It is part of how we chill out after the stress of work; it is signified by a personal and private construction which caters to our need for choice and our individual desires.

The Church as Past Times

The story is also interesting because it also underlines some contemporary views about the Christian Church. The Church may be seen as a thing of the past; it is being dismantled and given away. Parts of the Church's common heritage and history end up in people's personal and private domains. The furnishings of a corporate worshipping community pass into private hands and their history is discontinued and, ultimately, lost. Things which carry powerful sacramental significance for Christian believers, such as the water of baptism, the wood of the cross and the stone of the altar, lose these significances, resume their elemental life and pass into a private aesthetic. Consequently, we can now buy 'church candles' in supermarkets or buy 'spiritual' bath oil. Beyond such a contemporary spirituality, Christian heritage becomes part of an indulgence in nostalgia.[1] The *Past Times* Christmas catalogue invites purchasers to participate in the glories of a long ago Christmas: 'the finishing touch is always a traditional Christmas tree angel dressed in fine fabrics. Placed on the very top of the tree, such decorations commemorate the host of heavenly angels that appeared over the lowly stable in Bethlehem celebrating the first Christmas'.[2] The scriptural story becomes part of the promotional blurb to potential customers; the attraction is its appeal to the past, not as a living reality. This is a challenge to us, because the perception that the Church is outdated and only a piece of heritage can cast both clergy and churchgoing lay people in the role of custodians of the museum, preserving treasures of something which is no longer immediately relevant to people's lives.[3] Some people who like the idea of a traditional church wedding come with the view that it is part of an ancient custom, along with the antique car and clutch of quaint superstitions, and are surprised to be told that Christian vows before the living God can and should have an active reality in their marriage.

People are therefore encouraged to use their wealth to purchase material goods and services which form a constructed personal spirituality. Their spirituality is therefore about 'feeling good', creating 'well-being', a sense of 'connectedness' or 'transcendence', often in vague and unfocused ways. Personal possessions must be accrued and displayed in ways which maximize a person's sense of what is 'good' or what makes them 'happy'. Books on Feng Shui, for example, give guidance on maximizing this sense of spiritual 'rightness', or 'harmony'. Sometimes this involves ritual and a deliberate acquisition of possessions which ward off evil and represent the person's desire to stay on the side of the good. New Age shops particularly cater for this, with a variety of crystals, dream catchers, 'magical' figures and other attractive artefacts which signify a desire to stay safe, well and contented. We can argue that these things represent a surface spirituality which suffices until people encounter events in daily life for which these artefacts, rituals and practices have no comfort or answer. In the face of tragedy, illness, or other uncontrollable events, people often then turn to the Church as the only remaining place where answers can be found.[4] This does not mean that they then abandon the things which have had meaning for them and it may be a complex task to help people work through their implicit religious needs before inviting them to respond to the gospel. In order to make sense of this process, we need to understand what the difference is between such a constructed 'surface' spirituality and what we may mean or expect by the term 'spirituality' for ourselves.

Christian understanding of spirituality

This is not a simple matter, since, although many people use the word 'spiritual' or 'spirituality',[5] these can end up being very slippery terms used to mean a variety of different things. This is especially true if we are talking about a surface spirituality, which describes an ambience or a personal life path or an urge to stay on the side of the good. For Christians however, the deep structure of 'spirituality' can be more closely linked to fundamental questions about value, meaning and purpose. The questions hold true both for ourselves as individuals called by God and for the Body of Christ as a worshipping community. Such questions include:

- existential and ontological apperceptions of being 'in being'*(who am I?; why am I?)*;
- orientation of will *(what am I for?)*;
- moral orientation *(how shall I think/act?)*;
- relational consciousness[6] *(who shares my being in being?)*;
- view of ultimate destiny *(where am I going?)*.

How these questions are answered, both individually and corporately, depends on faith development filtered and changed by a number of factors. These can include:

- foundational knowledge and experience (including exposure to Church culture and knowledge of scripture and the Christian tradition);
- awareness of and response to 'an other' (including the capacity both to be alone with God and with God in community);
- cultural conditions (including the socio-political environment nationally and the local community or family environment);
- psychopathological factors, personality types.

We may argue that the deep structure of Christian spirituality, though it is worked out in different ways, tends to prompt people to consider what wider effects their faith and actions might have in the world. For this reason, we can argue that spirituality is at the heart of mission, fuelling a wish for transformation of unjust structures and feeding a desire to see justice and peace. The outworking of Christian spirituality should therefore have an active role in the missionary transformation of community. It is less easy to see this in the contemporary spirituality of people outside the church, although energy is often channelled into deeply felt causes.

The problem is that people growing up outside the faith tradition may themselves ask and form answers to the big questions cited above, but for them the answers offered by the Christian faith and lived out by Christians in the world are likely to be less and less adopted, even if they have the opportunity to hear the gospel. This is a challenge to our mission and asks serious questions of our evangelism. Do we, as Christians, *expect* certain types of answer in response to the big questions and can we cope with the alternative forms of discourse which may be offered to us? We may also take for granted a certain level of commitment, which for us is generated by the deep structure of our spirituality, but which others cannot and will not match.

Refusal to listen

A couple who brought their daughter for baptism were asked to attend a series of baptism preparation classes. At the classes, they came hoping to share with others the powerful sense of God's presence they had both experienced at the birth of their daughter and how this had sustained them while she had been in a Special Care Baby Unit. For them, the baptism was a confirmation that she was intended to live and have a future, and that they were offering to others the intense love and gratitude they felt. Unfortunately, they discovered that their story was of no interest to the people leading the class, and their motives were considered suspect because they were not churchgoers. They found the baptism preparation frustrating and distressing, because they felt that the other people thought they were somehow 'not qualified' to speak of God.

Similarly, in *The Spirit of the Child*,[7] David Hay and Rebecca Nye reported children's spiritual experiences of God being corrected, dismissed or overwritten by adults, because the events were not reported in language which fitted the 'orthodox' picture of a 'genuine' encounter with God. The result was that often, powerful experiences of God, both of presence and of call, were locked down into a silent space in the child's mind and heart, which were only released in the safe space created by the researcher.[8]

These examples show that we ourselves may make it more difficult to engage with the spirituality of people outside the church and that we may lay down the terms for a commitment which others cannot fulfil.

Loss of Christian tradition and knowledge

In order to respond sensitively to the spirituality of people outside the Church, we have to be aware of the deficits in people's lives. We may assume that people interact with us on the same knowledge base as ourselves and that we share similar understanding and experience. But it is clear that in today's society people may be much less likely to go to church or have members of their family for whom churchgoing was a tradition; they are less likely to learn and absorb Christian prayers, hymns and Bible stories; they are also less likely to receive statements of Christian truth-claims at an early age – neither of simple catechetical statements of the 'who made you? God made me' type, nor of the historic creeds.

This loss of encounter with foundational Christian metanarrative and epistemology means that there may be a lack of reference points for people to use, adapt (or rebel against) in forming satisfactory answers to big questions. Where such gaps occur, people find material to fill them and where such material does not come from a foundational authority (e.g. a major world religion), things may be left fuzzy, vague, mystical or secret (gnostic). People literally shop around for material to fill the void and retailers happily oblige. This may result in a 'pick and mix' selection of religious ideas and practices in which people may move from one religious allegiance to another in the course of their search. A particular example of this occurs in response to the question 'where am I going?' where people with apparently quite orthodox Christian understanding will suggest that they will be reincarnated on earth in some way or have to take steps to counteract 'bad karma'.

The Mission Theological Advisory Group has argued that there are some particular sociological factors in contemporary western society which affect people's spiritual journeys and condition its overt expression.[9] If we are to understand and to respond to contemporary spirituality effectively, we need to be aware of these factors which also operate in our own lives.

Some sociological phenomena affecting people's lives today

The first of these is individualization. This process in society prompts people to value self-worth to the exclusion of the worth of all others. Individualization drives the need continually to have choice and constantly to revise choice decisions. The individualized person constructs a life from the best possible choices available and without recourse to the needs or wants of other people. The L'Oreal slogan is 'because you're worth it'. The self becomes privileged as a matter of right. So we should not think it strange when we read in the press of a mother who went on holiday leaving her small children locked alone in her flat. She explained that she 'needed the holiday'. Individualization can therefore erode notions of community and responsibility. It is someone's else's job to care. The singer Sonique, who thanks on her first album cover 'the man above through the good times and bad' nonetheless said in the '60 second interview' column of the London *Metro* newspaper: 'My whole life is about me and my existence, not what other people think I should appreciate'.[10] We should not be surprised, then, to find individualized spirituality being constructed to enhance a private sense of self over against an understanding of the place and purpose of self in fellowship or in community.

The phenomenon of post-materialism works hand in hand with individualization. This phenomenon gives acquired objects status beyond their utility. This is very clear in the case of things like cars and mobile phones. A car is not just a machine which ferries a person from A to B, but its colour, size, accessories and extras are descriptive to others of who the driver/owner is. Your mobile phone is not a communication device, but its functions, clip-on covers, ring tones and accessories send signals to those around you about the kind of person you are. Things are acquired for what they say about their owners and multiplicity of choice drives them into uniqueness, the tailor-made and the multi-function. Post-materialism also means that material things are superseded quickly by better and more up-to-date versions of themselves, leading to a quick turnover, disposable culture and throw-away attitude towards possessions. Indeed, the utility of things may be the least attractive feature. One advertisement for a Siemens washing machine is not that it washes well but that 'I can wash my knickers in 15 different languages'. Spirituality therefore also becomes a fashion victim and celebrities' spiritual interests (such as Madonna's interest in Kabbalah) become part of the image that others may copy. People may therefore hop from one set of religious ideas and practices to others or try out different kinds of belief system. What happens then, when we, as Christians, encounter those 'trying out' Christianity with one eye on ditching Jesus Christ as soon as he fails to please? What attitude do we take towards those whose Christianity is part of their overall image?

The third factor which affects people's lives is globalization. Manifestly, globalization has many differing effects, but one perspective to which people are constantly exposed is the idea that markets cannot be bucked and that we have little control about what happens to money. House prices may rocket and shares may fall yet there seems little to be done about it. The sensible option is therefore to give in to the pressures of individualization and spend the money on a short-term future. People are actively encouraged not to think about their money as a gift or a responsibility but to realize it as quickly as possible into post-material acquisitions – a holiday of a lifetime, a new car. Spending power is therefore channelled into the individualized life and people may spend what they earn on their constructed spirituality – feel-good therapies and practices, or the dream holiday as a kind of pilgrimage. Any sense that we are building God's future becomes contracted to the possibilities of one lifetime, so that sacrifice for others seems irrational and pointless.

In such an environment, the concept of something which is offered freely without prior investment or financial promise may seem impossible or entirely suspicious. How, then, can Christians offer the free gift of Christ's love and the promise of salvation to people who do not know how to accept it? Moreover, how far are we responsible for the popular perception that the Church is always after a person's money?

Along with all of these other phenomena, we encounter more and more the fact that people may carry a number of diverse ideas in their heads, some of which may actually conflict with each other. Such conceptual diversity may be the result of incomplete answers to big questions, or the adoption of parts of different sense-making systems. These different assertions of belief may only be revealed to different interlocutors. For example, a person may tell a minister that s/he believes everything the Church teaches, but tell their doctor about the use of crystals or other New Age healing devices. To yet others, s/he may reveal deeply reductionist or fatalistic convictions.

> A woman whose husband died told her parish priest that she believed all the Church teaches about the afterlife and appeared comforted by her pastoral care. However, she shortly afterwards told her doctor that she believed that when we die, we rot and that there is nothing else. She said she felt depressed and hopeless and asked for medication. On yet another occasion, she said that she felt the spirit of her husband was still around the house and trying to indicate to her that there were things which still had to be put right.

While psychological factors and the work of grief undoubtedly played a part in this case, it is clear that different fragments of belief and thought had different outcomes and generated different responses and requirements. The challenge to Christians is that we may assume that the response we look for and receive is the only thing going on in people's heads and unless we are willing to receive other stories and ideas, even conflicting ones, we may never know what else is happening in the construction of others' spirituality.

Emerging themes in contemporary spirituality

Another problem in understanding contemporary spirituality is that Christians may not affirm or endorse the strong underlying impulses to stay on the side of the good and to keep away from the bad. *The Search for Faith and the Witness of the Church* showed this at work in people's responses to questions about their spirituality.[11] The themes which emerged included:

- *a desire to be in control of one's spiritual journey.* This means that spirituality is an expression of a personal contract between the self and God and is not conditioned or affected by the life of the worshipping community. People may look for role models, but not for spiritual directors or guides.
- *to feel good about one's body, one's self and one's sexuality.* The perception here is that the Church is incoherent about what it means to be a human being. People feel that the Church generally frowns on matters of embodiment and especially on sexuality, so that delight in human creatureliness becomes a matter of guilt and secrecy.

evidence

- *to have some immediate hope in and for the future.* People want short term hope, which is tailor made to their needs (so personal astrological charts can often fit the bill) not an overarching big picture which includes everyone.
- *to feel in harmony with the natural world.* People perceive the Church to be incoherent about its creation theology and unclear about human relations to the planet and to animals. Sometimes people construct their spirituality entirely around green issues and are drawn to New Age or green or environment-friendly practices in order to express this sense of care and love for the creation.

By contrast, Hay and Hunt showed that people believe the Church wants to have the control – that men, especially, believe the Church to be preoccupied with negative or punitive feelings about sin and judgement, that the Church is preoccupied with living in the past and that the Church does not take notice of numinous feelings or experiences of nature. Despite a general goodwill towards Christians and Christian faith, the popular perception of Church may therefore be that it is in conflict with spiritual growth and development.

These responses show that people outside the Church do not wait for our input, but make choices for their spiritual development, rejecting anything that does not fit their lifestyle options. They may also postpone decisions about ultimate destiny, and may pay for practices and therapies, including psychotherapy and counselling. For example, Princess Diana, as a famous personality idolized and copied by many, and seen as a 'spiritual' person, was known to undertake body therapies such as colonic irrigation, to consult an astrologer and seek out healing and relaxation therapies and mental stress-relieving practices. People may pay a great deal of attention to the efficacy of things they eat and drink[12] and search out more holistic solutions to their sense of dissatisfaction or lack of peace. They may seek out quick-fix, short-term solutions to design[13] their living and their hope for the future. This means they shorten their horizons and set up anthropomorphic pictures of otherness, with many fewer, and distorted, apperceptions of a transcendental or indeed eschatological reality. This leads to a fascination and even preoccupation with UFOs, ghosts, vampires, angels etc.[14] Moral and ethical questions are not a matter of right living in community, but of individual behaviour, which may have vestigial religious elements which find their way into popular programmes such as soap operas and medical dramas. These are often picked up and turned into big issues by the media.

Problems with what the Church offers

Contemporary spirituality also demonstrates that the Christian tradition, its doctrine, expression in worship and the Church's self-understanding and expectations may be very far from people's spiritual pathways. In particular:

- Christian faith is offered to any kind of person of any age and requires facing unpleasantness, such as sin, suffering, judgement and death (but society is concerned with short-termism and feeling good);
- it is for the whole community, dedicated to God's Kingdom, and therefore has moral implications (but society is individualized);
- it is concerned with ultimate destiny and the question of salvation (but people postpone their decisions and often find the Church is not there when they come back to ultimate questions);
- it privileges those without choices, elevating the weak and the powerless (but society sees choice as a right);
- it places demands and obligations and asks for commitment to a set of foundational truths, with particular reference to the divinity and humanity of Jesus (but society engages in relativistic processes and pick and mix spiritualities);
- it has a self-understanding beyond and sometimes over against contemporary culture (but society likes to go with the flow and to engage in an easy tolerance of almost anything);
- it has an orientation which is subject to the will and intention of a missionary God (but society likes to retain its control).

The advantage of some Christian basics courses, such as *Alpha*, is that they set the Christian paradigm out clearly and unequivocally. A problem is that for many people seeking for 'spiritual truth', the Christian tradition is either alien or anathema to the way they envisage their spiritual development. They may be very anti-institutional or view the Church as hypocritical. People say 'I'm spiritual, but not religious' or 'I'm a Christian, but I don't go to Church'.

Appropriation of Christian material and themes

Another phenomenon associated with contemporary expressions of spirituality, and one which Christians must address, is the tendency for people to take parts of Christian tradition and change or adapt it for their personal spirituality. There are many examples of this, but we can take just one example which has a popular currency: angels. In contemporary spirituality, the idea of the angel has been taken over into a personalized watcher or guardian, a sort of heavenly personal trainer. The pop singer Robbie Williams' *Angels*, for example, is not only a hit, but now one of the most covered songs. Now it is finding its way into marriage services and funerals as people request it as being meaningful to them:

> And through it all, she offers me protection, a lot of love and affection, whether I'm right or wrong ... I look above and I know I'll always be blessed with love.

In this song, the idea of angel as lover, guardian, protector, preserver, model of faithfulness and healer of sorrows, is annexed to the usual ballad of human love. Interestingly he brings in the word 'salvation', both as the rescue from a bad relationship but also perhaps (but only perhaps) as something more. The idea of the protecting angel is common in pop music ballads and appears also in films such as *City of Angels*. The enormously popular American TV series *Buffy the Vampire Slayer* also nicely turns the tradition on its head, by naming one of its most dangerous monsters Angel. Books, too, find angels a powerful presence, from Golding's *Darkness Visible* to Gaarder's *Through a Glass Darkly* and Coupland's *Girlfriend in a Coma*.

Angels are a powerful presence in the Bible, in other world religions, and in the European tradition of religious painting. Angels are messengers of God, agents of testing, bringers of God's retribution and justice, eternal worshippers and representations of God's own self (the angel of the presence). But in the flood of material on the Internet, we can find the idea of 'angels' being annexed to lighting candles for petitions, dreams, wishes, affecting outcomes; colours and associated emotion states; astrological signs and days of the week as well as parts of the body and eastern healing practices.

For example, *Sarah's Archangels*, a very attractive pagan/wiccan Internet site,[15] suggests that the Angel Gabriel:

> is the Governor of the West and the element of Water. Ruler of Monday, psychic gifts, intuition, visions, magick, clairvoyance, scrying, astral travel, herbal medicine, the cycles of women, and females aspects of men. His symbols are the lily and the trumpet, and his stone is the moonstone.

> Gabriel's candle colours are silver, white and blue.

> Gabriel's colour energies are white, silver, rose, blue, crystal, and scarlet.

> Invoke Gabriel in the west for stronger powers of intuition and psychic gifts.

We are also told that the Archangel Gabriel is the patron saint of telecommunications. Angels are seen as an integral part of an holistic spiritual practice which includes harmonization of physical, mental, emotional and spiritual states. There is a recontextualization of biblical ideas and material into something more locally holistic for personal use. Beyond this, there is the commercial aspect so necessary to the individualized, post-material society. The site allows you to shop for the angel accoutrements which best fit your lifestyle.

Responding to the challenge

The spirituality of people outside the Church challenges us because it reminds us that we do not own the work of the Holy Spirit. Often we can become preoccupied with the idea that God somehow only exists to validate the life and actions of the Church.[16] If we are to respond to God in Christ however, we have to be aware that we can all too easily become part of the problem, reinforcing people's ideas of the hypocrisy and general irrelevance of the Church.

We might remember, however, that Jesus himself had to deal with the challenges of the prevailing spirituality in a particular cultural environment. He did this by addressing fundamental assumptions about practice and challenging them (e.g. contravening the Sabbath); by dealing with moral questions (tax, adultery); by re-visioning God's Kingdom in terms of God's equality and option for the poor and weak and by refocusing minds on an eschatological reality. The course of Jesus' ministry: teaching, healing, and performing significant actions provides us with models for seeing mission as a countercultural activity and as a prophetic mode for addressing contemporary spirituality.

The task is therefore to allow refocusing but not supplanting of people's spiritual instincts and desires. This refocusing can include helping people see beyond their self-interest by pointing to God's option for the poor; directing people to a God who suffers with us and providing clarity in theodicy. We may also need to ask people to consider God's moral equality and Kingdom issues for the whole community, pointing to God's forgiveness and eternal love as a free gift and reminding people of God's desire to reconcile the whole creation.

This means that we also have to be challenged and changed by the insights of people outside the Church. It requires speaking into and receiving from others' stories of faith development and spiritual growth, recovering a rich language of God and allowing people to articulate their own faith,[17] accompanying people in their faith journeys[18] and challenging assumptions and presuppositions inside and outside the Church.

We cannot make any progress in understanding the spirituality of people outside the Church if we remain silent on difficult issues and questions and avoid the challenge, which may expose unpleasant truths about ourselves. We cannot afford to be patronizing or to rewrite people's experience in terms we find more comfortable. Often we use our research and statistics to support the idea that our view of the world still somehow prevails, without looking at how that view is often being dismantled and reconstructed for different purposes outside our city walls. If we want to engage with it effectively and prophetically, we have to leave our safe havens and risk the challenges to our comfortable faith.

NOTES

1. But David Hay and Kate Hunt point to the powerful emotions sometimes evinced by the nostalgic and which we may miss. There can be mission opportunities at even the most sentimental infant nativity play, where longings for a time when Good News was announced, and 'when all was well', rise to the surface. See Hay, David and Hunt, Kate, *Understanding the Spirituality of People who Don't Go to Church* (Nottingham University, Centre for the Study of Human Relations, 2000, p. 33).
2. *Past Times*, Christmas Catalogue 2001, p. 9.
3. So the Cardinal Archbishop of Westminster described his fear that Christian faith is 'vanquished' and the former Archbishop of Canterbury has also remarked that for many young people Christianity is simply irrelevant.
4. So after the 11 September tragedies and the Soham murders, people came to churches to lay flowers, say prayers and light candles.
5. In their research, Hay and Hunt noted that for many people 'spirituality' is associated with 'spiritualism' or other occult practice: *Understanding the Spirituality of People who Don't Go to Church*, pp. 24–5.
6. David Hay and Rebecca Nye use this phrase to denote innate awareness of an other: *The Spirit of the Child* (HarperCollins 1998). It is also described in *Understanding the Spirituality of People who Don't Go to Church*.
7. See, for example, *The Spirit of the Child*, p. 102.
8. See also 'Tom's' story in *Understanding the Spirituality of People who Don't Go to Church*, pp. 20–3.
9. Mission Theological Advisory Group, *The Search for Faith and the Witness of the Church* (Church House Publishing 1996), pp. 19–22; Mission Theological Advisory Group, *Presence and Prophecy: a Heart for Mission in Theological Education* (Church House Publishing 2002), chapter 1. Also see for comparison the Revd Dr Michael Moynagh's work in *Changing World, Changing Church*, (Monarch/Administry 2001).
10. *Metro* (12 September 2000).
11. *The Search for Faith and the Witness of the Church*, chapter 3, pp. 74–109.
12. This is not just calorie counting, but a preoccupation with putting 'good' things into the body and driving out 'bad' things, such as 'toxins' and damaging 'free radicals'.
13. The importance of the 'designer' function as part of people's control and

shaping of their lives cannot be underestimated. Hence the proliferation of 'design' programmes about health and beauty, interiors, gardens and cooking on TV.

14. Hay and Hunt showed that more people than ever before reported an awareness of evil or a feeling of the presence of the dead: *Understanding the Spirituality of People who Don't Go to Church*, pp. 13–14.

15. http://www.sarahsarchangels.com

16. See Walter Brueggemann's argument in *The Prophetic Imagination* (Fortress Press 1978), p. 43.

17. Hay and Hunt emphasize the fact that people mention fear of embarrassment or of being humiliated or laughed at by card-carrying Christians and may lock up their experiences and confide them to nobody: *Understanding the Spirituality of People who Don't Go to Church*, pp. 35–6.

18. Again, Hay and Hunt refer to the importance of sacred space, which we may take for granted: *Understanding the Spirituality of People who Don't Go to Church*, p. 32.

7

Is Britain a Christian Country?

David Voas

We have an idea of what it means, personally, to be Christian. For many of us, evidently, it is a rather hazy idea. Still, some beliefs and ideals and customs mark people out as Christian. Can we apply the term not just to people, though, but to *a* people, for example the British people? And does it make sense to talk about a Christian country? We need to consider what that might mean, and whether Britain qualifies.

In broad historical terms, Britain is manifestly Christian. The marks can be seen as easily on the law and literature as on the landscape. The imprint is not merely Christian but more specifically denominational: England, Scotland and Wales seem to bear the imprint of church, kirk and chapel respectively. Of course nothing is pure – here and there one may discern the remnants of paganism, or see a direct influence of Judaism or Buddhism – but to the extent that religion has shaped our culture, it is the Christian heritage that is almost solely relevant. The key question is how far to credit (blame?) religion for what we have, and have become. No doubt there are Christian overtones in any number of present-day songs, films, social movements and public policies, but purely secular influences now seem more important. The world our great-grandparents inherited was Christian in a way that the one we inhabit is not.

The long-running debate about how, when, why and even whether secularization has occurred in the West is bedevilled by the difficulty of measuring religious adherence. Partly in consequence scholars have disagreed about what there is to explain, as well as which explanations best suit whatever the facts might be. To take a few recent examples, Rodney Stark claims that secularization is a myth, Callum Brown argues that in Britain it only started in the early 1960s but is now virtually complete, Grace Davie holds that Europe is an exception and that even here religiosity persists in altered forms, while Steve Bruce defends a classical perspective that finds the seeds of secularization as far back as the

Reformation, with the fruits being evident from at least the mid-nineteenth century.

Some of these difficulties could be avoided by focusing on society rather than on persons, bearing in mind Bryan Wilson's standard definition of secularization: the decline in the social significance of religion. Even so, however, it is hard to assess the impact of religion on society without a reasonable understanding of its role in individual lives. Let us revert, then, to looking at people. We know, of course, that many Britons are not in any sense Christian, except to the extent that we are all also in some degree Jews and Muslims and humanists insofar as we share certain core values. What we are trying to decide, though, is not whether affiliation is universal, but rather whether it is characteristic. Perhaps Britain is Christian in the way that particular districts might have been classed as farming or mining areas, not because everyone there did those things but because the activities were important enough to make the descriptions apt.

What does it mean to have a religion?

Personal identity is anything but simple. Cosmopolitan visitors to less developed countries will be bemused by questions about their 'native place': to someone in a traditional society, coming from such-and-such village may be of the utmost importance, while to increasing numbers of Westerners it is more or less incidental where they were born or grew up. Likewise with religion: origins may mean a lot or a little. Most Europeans are still able to specify their religious background, just as they can name their birthplace, father's occupation and secondary school, but whether these things make any difference to how they see themselves or the way they are perceived by others is not at all certain. The study of changing levels of religious adherence thus raises a double problem: first to try to measure some sense of belonging, and secondly to decide what the results might mean.

There is no single marker of having a religion. A number of factors may be relevant: belief, practice, membership, affiliation, ritual initiation, cultural affinity, moral sense, basic ideology, external perception, or something else. 'Being religious' is not easily definable or directly observable. It is a multi-dimensional quality for which we have various indicators, but no real measure. Even with the scales decided there are problems, particularly when we want to compare religiosity over time and cross-nationally. Can we devise consistent indicators that go back decades or centuries, and that apply in different societies? And if different indicators seem to tell different stories, what should we infer?

Church statistics and national surveys provide data on active participa-tion, especially attendance at worship. There are also data on what proportion of the population accepts various religious beliefs. Neither belief nor practice, however, necessarily coincides with the personal sense of *being* Anglican or Catholic or Muslim or Jewish. Membership in a straightforward voluntary association lapses without continued participation (or at least subscription). While churches may be on the road to functioning like Amnesty or the WI, religion for the present is still capable of being an aspect of personal identity that does not depend on active involvement, official membership or even agreement with basic doctrine. In these circumstances religious affiliation may seem more meaningful than the more overt signs of faith or participation. Let us be systematic, though, considering levels of religious activity and then belief before moving to affiliation.

Activity

To judge purely by church attendance Britain is not very Christian, nor is Christian England very Anglican. The best estimate for Sunday church attendance in Great Britain in 2000 was just below eight per cent of the population.[1] Only about a quarter of those attending in England are worshipping in the Church of England; they are substantially outnumbered by Catholics at mass. To foreshadow a theme of this chapter, it must be said that statistics on attendance are not nearly as clear-cut as one might like. For a start, Sunday is not the only day people may choose to go to church, and the Church of England has recently tried to focus on a broader measure of attendance that includes mid-week services.

More importantly, the number of *people* attending regularly is of greater interest than the number of *visits* to church. If all churchgoers went exactly once every four weeks, then having eight percent of the population in church on a given Sunday would translate into a third of the population worshipping each month. In fact the 'multiplier' of weekly attendance needed to arrive at the churchgoing total is not as large as four, but it is substantial: perhaps between two and three. The level of religious activity is both low by past standards and declining – there is no escaping the bad news – but it is not as depressed as might at first blush appear.

In past times monthly attendance would have been condemned as lax; now it might be welcomed as a sign of reasonable constancy. Even if we were able to arrive at a figure for 'regular' churchgoers (a task that is far from easy), one has the problem of interpreting the slide towards less frequent attendance. Is it the regularity or the frequency that is significant? People who attend church of their own volition, however occasionally, are no doubt showing some signs of religious feeling; that said, it is hard to avoid judging the strength of those feelings by the level of associated activity, at least in the aggregate.

As a final comment on attendance, it is surprisingly difficult to obtain accurate estimates from what people say that they do. A celebrated, if controversial, contribution to the scholarly literature on religion in the United States compared self-reported attendance from polls with actual counts of people in church, and found very substantial discrepancies.[2] A similar phenomenon can be seen in Britain. A 1999 Gallup poll posing the question 'How often do you go to church?' generated responses that appear somewhat inflated relative to church survey data.[3] Similarly, asking people what they did the previous weekend, offering a list that includes home improvement, visiting friends and other possibilities in addition to churchgoing, results in a figure some 50 per cent higher than actual attendance. Even more surprisingly, enquiring whether the individual attended within the last seven days (the question normally used in American Gallup polls) has produced values that are more than twice as high as observed weekly attendance.[4]

There are important lessons here for pollsters. A question that seems absolutely precise, to which one can give an unambiguous yes/no response, is being interpreted as something far more complex. As Hadaway and Marler point out, when Gallup asks 'Did you, yourself, happen to attend church or synagogue in the last seven days?', they make the respondent symbolically choose between being churched and unchurched. If being a churchgoer is part of one's personal identity, there may be considerable resistance to answering in a way that places one outside the fold. Clearly subjective feelings of regularity are being translated into unrealistic frequencies; what one might infer about religiosity is an interesting but complicated matter.

Belief

One much-discussed suggestion is that Britain is characterized by 'believing without belonging',[5] i.e. that religious (and at least approximately Christian) beliefs are still generally held, but that active involvement in church is confined to a small minority. This interpretation of affairs is perhaps the leading domestic example of the 'Third Way' in the sociology of religion, offering an alternative to both a standard secularization approach (that would stress the diminishing social significance of religion) and the persistence view (according to which the amount of religion is not so different now than in the past, though it may take new forms: in effect a law of conservation of religious energy). The thesis might imply that the best measure of adherence is in fact some expression of belief rather than of institutional membership or practice.

Opinion polls in this country do indeed show high levels of belief, but in all sorts of things, including reincarnation (a quarter of respondents), horoscopes (also a quarter), clairvoyance (almost half), ghosts (nearly a third) and so on.[6] It is far from clear that these beliefs make any difference to the people claiming them. Research suggests that casual believers even in astrology, for example, which is distinguished by its practical orientation, rarely do or avoid doing things because of published advice.[7] Studies on polling show that people are prepared to express opinions about almost anything, whether or not they have any knowledge of or interest in the topic. The upshot is a phenomenon one might call 'believing without believing'. Views are uninformed, not deeply held, seldom acted upon, and relatively volatile. People may feel that on certain matters they are required to hold and even to express opinions, but that is not the same as finding those issues particularly important.

While 25 per cent of respondents may say that they believe in reincarnation, one is not inclined to feel that they thereby express any basic truths about their own identities. The corollary, though, is that it is difficult to be too impressed by the apparent number of conventional believers. I am not arguing here that the large subpopulation that acknowledges the God of our fathers – the memorably styled 'ordinary God'[8] – is shallow or insincere. My point is simply that we cannot conclude from the fact that people tell pollsters they believe in God that they give the matter any thought, find it significant, will feel the same next year, or plan to do anything about it.

In any event one can no longer infer from the widespread inclination to believe in a broadly-defined God that people are basically Christian. Opinion polls over recent decades suggest (even given the previous caveats about interpreting survey evidence) that the characteristically Christian beliefs – particularly in Jesus as the Son of God – have been in decline, and are now held by a minority.[9] Many Britons would like to be known as 'spiritual' (the alternatives seem unattractive; who wants to be labelled a 'materialist'?) and will therefore acknowledge a belief in something, but that something is less and less likely to be Christ.

A useful supplementary approach (employed for example by Opinion Research Business in its Soul of Britain survey) is to ask respondents to rate the personal importance of various activities they might have tried, from prayer to divination. Similar questions can be found on some national surveys; the British Household Panel Study, for example, periodically asks 'How much difference would you say religious beliefs make to your life?' The responses are enormously helpful in distinguishing between real commitment and mild interest or nominal allegiance.

Connecting what people say (particularly in answer to survey questions) with what they believe is not always easy. It is still far from clear, moreover, that beliefs will necessarily enter into personal identity. If we want to measure the place of religion in self-definition, it is best to tackle the issue directly.

Formal affiliation

The most objective test is also in some ways the most valid, to wit, whether baptized individuals represent more or less than half the population. There is no doubt that by this definition Britain is still, quite comfortably, a Christian country. It is equally evident that on present trends it will not remain so.

Among people over fifty years of age in England, around 70 per cent were baptized by the Church of England. By the mid-1970s, however, the Church was baptizing fewer than half of all infants, and in 2000 the proportion of newborns christened as Anglicans dropped below one in five.[10] Although some of the remainder are baptized as children or later in life, up to three-quarters of the current English generation will avoid even ceremonial induction into the official church. It is worth noting, however, that baptism is not the only service on offer to parents: thanksgiving is available as an alternative.

By doing a careful year-by-year calculation of births, baptisms, mortality, migration, and so on, I was recently able to arrive at a good estimate of the notionally Anglican (as defined by christening) population. In 2001 this group dropped below 50 per cent of the total number of British subjects living in England. For the first time since the Church was founded, then, nominal adherents of the established faith are in a minority. England is no longer an Anglican country.

The church is losing a million baptized Anglicans every five years as they die without being replaced. Losses will continue at that level for at least three decades, unless there is a dramatic resurgence in the popularity of christening. By the end of the century the notionally Anglican community will be less than half the size that it is today, even assuming there are no further declines in baptism rates. Given its age structure relative to the younger profile of other Christian groups, the Church of England is also likely to have a diminishing share of the total baptized population.

It appears unlikely, however, that baptism rates will stabilize at present levels. For more than half a century now the probability of a child being christened has been approximately equal to the probability that both of its parents are at least nominal Anglicans. If that formula continues to hold, the rate of C of E baptism twenty years from now will be below ten per cent. To use an analogy from heredity, religious affiliation is acting like a recessive gene: it only appears in the new generation if the parents supply a matching pair.[11] Churches aiming for a revival of adherence would need to address these problems of transmission rather than simply focusing on adult conversion.

The Church of England is only one church, of course, even if the most important in size and constitutional status. There are reasons to believe that Christian initiation will be important for some time yet. In the Soul of Britain Survey, 53 per cent of respondents stated a desire for a service marking birth. The figure had fallen from 65 per cent in 1990, and was lower than the proportion desiring a ceremony for marriage or death. It is still somewhat higher than the levels currently seeking christening, which might be related to the generational differences discussed below. It might also be a sign of the perplexity expressed by the footballer David Beckham, who has said 'I definitely want Brooklyn to be christened ... but I don't know into what religion yet'.[12] People may be interested in a ritual for initiation into some longed-for community, without feeling particularly drawn to the options currently on offer.

Although Davie[13] puts both Church of England and other baptisms at 25 per cent of infants each, the non-Anglican estimate seems overly generous. In England, Catholics contribute no more than 11 per cent and Methodists another 3.5 per cent.[14] Even adding the United Reformed Church, Orthodox, etc., and indeed Baptists and others who do not practise infant baptism, it is clear that the total for all Christian churches falls well short of 50 per cent. The denominational distribution will be different in Scotland and Wales, but not the general picture. Short of a religious revival, it is only a matter of time before Britain ceases to be a Christian country in the literal sense: baptized Christians will be in a minority.

Self-ascribed affiliation

A possible test of whether Britain is Christian is simply whether a majority of people claim to be such. Unfortunately the answers vary considerably depending on how and in what context one asks the question. At one extreme, for example, the 2001 Census of Population shows 72 per cent of people in England and Wales, and 65 per cent of those in Scotland, categorized as Christian. On the census form for England and Wales religion follows the questions on country of birth and ethnicity, so that it appears (reflecting the intentions expressed in the census White Paper) to be a supplementary question on the same topic.[15] The positive phraseology ('What is your religion?') combined with tick-box options that simply list world religions (e.g. Christian/Muslim/Hindu) invite the respondent to specify a cultural background rather than a current affiliation. Note too that census forms are typically completed by the household head on behalf of all individuals at the address, and to the extent that such persons tend to be older and more religious than average, the numbers may be higher than they would be on confidential individual questionnaires. The religion question used on the census form in Scotland preceded (rather than followed) those on ethnicity, and also offered answer categories for specific Christian denominations; perhaps as a result, people were nearly twice as likely as in England to give their affiliation as 'none'.

In contrast to the census, the question posed in the British Social Attitudes (BSA) survey occurs in the context of a wide-ranging enquiry into opinion and practice, and is worded in a way that might seem more likely to discourage than to encourage a positive response ('Do you regard yourself as belonging to any particular religion?'). The respondent must interpret for him or herself what 'belonging' might mean, but for most it probably implies some current as opposed to past affiliation. Indeed, the BSA questionnaire goes on to ask what religion (if any) one was brought up in, and the answers are strikingly different. While some 40 per cent of people in 2000 and 2001 said that they belonged to no religion, only a quarter as many declared that they had been raised without one. A bare majority still present themselves as belonging to a Christian denomination.

The importance of wording is strikingly apparent when we compare the BSA results with those from Gallup Polls. In the latter the question has a strong positive presumption, similar to that found in the recent census: 'What is your religious denomination?' In consequence the proportion of 'nones' is less than half that found in BSA survey: 18 per cent in 1993, as against 39 per cent in 1994 from the BSA survey. Fully a fifth of people apparently do not regard themselves as *belonging* to a particular religion, but if pushed to claim one will do so. Even nominal affiliation has different levels: in conjunction with the phenomenon of 'believing without believing', there are multiple ways of 'belonging without belonging'. Relatively few people actually practise their supposed religion; there is much more notional belonging than there is actual belonging.

A Gallup Poll conducted for the *Daily Telegraph* in November 1999 asked the question 'Would you describe yourself today as a Christian or non-Christian?' One imagines that many people might interpret non-Christian to mean an adherent of another religion, and one finds 64 per cent choosing 'Christian'. It would be interesting to know what would have been the responses to a question that simply asked 'Would you describe yourself as a Christian?' (which still allows the use of the term as a broad ethical label), or again 'Are you a Christian?' (where perhaps the implication of belonging is more pronounced; indeed, the query has evangelical overtones).

Obviously many of these notional Christians will not be churchgoers on even the broadest definition. Even the more demanding questions that solicit a denominational label will produce results substantially higher than actual membership or attendance levels might suggest. There is obviously a sense of belonging that rests on self-identification rather than any participation in church life. For a significant number of people religion is still more like a nationality (which you can have even if you live and pay taxes elsewhere) than a voluntary association (in which membership must be regularly renewed).

It is important to appreciate, however, that there is enormous variation by age in the extent of this kind of identification. Among people aged 65 and over surveyed for the BSA in 2001, 72 per cent say that they regard themselves as belonging to a Christian denomination, while only 31 per cent of young adults (18–24) so describe themselves. These differences may be influenced by life stage (older people being more religious than young ones), but the evidence suggests that in the main they are generational (a steady decline in religiosity over time). The Soul of Britain survey in 2000 was perhaps the first to show self-described Christians in an overall minority. In future such results – with the unaffiliated and non-Christians outnumbering declared Christians – will be increasingly common.

Is the state Christian?

Finally, Britain might be a Christian country in some official sense. The urge to associate religion with the nation has been apparent in many parts of the world, from Japan to India to Ireland to the United States. Britain is formally a religious country in a way that many modern states are not, having the established Church of England and the national Church of Scotland. There is a willingness to countenance religious involvement in the machinery of government: the Royal Commission on the Reform of the House of Lords chaired by Lord Wakeham even recommended that the number of religious seats in the upper house be increased from 26 to 31, though fewer of those would be Anglican bishops. In its subsequent White Paper the government did not accept the proposed representation of other religious groups, but neither did it suggest eliminating the bishops.

It would be facile, however, to point to the existence of an established church in England as 'proof' that we live in a Christian country. If the issue were merely one of definition then the links between church and state might settle the matter. In fact, however, these links have very little impact on contemporary life. In some cases they seem to achieve the worst of both worlds, creating an impression that offends one side without benefiting the other. The law on blasphemy, for example, seems to Muslims to show that the English deck is stacked in Christianity's favour, and yet the law is effectively a dead letter; it is almost inconceivable that a case could even be brought today, much less successfully prosecuted.

England is in the somewhat anomalous position of having an established church attended by only a minority of active churchgoers. The position is very different if one looks at affiliation rather than attendance, though there is still no direct connection between establishment and the size of the Anglican population. According to the BSA survey, some 29 per cent of adults regard themselves as belonging to the Anglican church. On the one hand this figure might seem rather low; after all, roughly half the adults in Britain were baptized by the C of E (or its sister churches in Wales and Scotland), and so would be entitled to identify themselves as Anglican. On the other hand the value is still higher than that for all other Christian denominations combined, or indeed for all other faiths combined (though only just).[16]

Once again there is an important generational factor. The Church of England does not enjoy the dominance among the young that it still holds – notionally, at least – among the old. At age 60+, Anglicans are in a clear majority of Christians (60 per cent); there are nearly five times as many Anglicans as Catholics and twice as many Anglicans as 'other Christians' (i.e. neither C of E nor RC). In the group 18–24 (admittedly a small sub-sample) there are equal numbers in each of the three groups, and even in the larger 25–34 group there are only twice as many Anglicans as Catholics, and one and a half times as many Anglicans as other Protestants, etc.

In these circumstances criticism of the special constitutional status of the Church of England is likely to continue. The Church of Ireland and then the Church in Wales were disestablished on the grounds that they served only a minority of the population. The argument is the same today, and the democratic principle (not to mention concern for minority rights) has more force now than it did in the nineteenth or early twentieth centuries. Although nothing is quick when considering ecclesiastical and constitutional change, it is hard not to foresee continuing erosion, if not outright abolition, of establishment. Interestingly a Deliberative Poll on the Monarchy conducted for Channel 4 in 1996 found that while only 26 per cent of the panel agreed when 'uninformed' that 'The Monarchy should not stay head of the Church of England', there was a dramatic jump to 56 per cent after assimilating and discussing expert presentation of the rival positions.

Of course the survival of establishment does not depend on the existence of a 'silent majority' that remains nominally Anglican. Debates on the issue are often curious affairs, with some bishops arguing that we should 'cut the connection' (the title of a book by the Rt Revd Colin Buchanan) and some

Muslims seeking to retain the Church as a bulwark against secularization. In these circumstances the special privileges and duties of the C of E have no obvious bearing on Britain's character as Christian or otherwise.

There are two aspects to national identity, though, as for personal identity: how we see ourselves, and how others see us. To the non-Western world Great Britain may appear to be a representative of a globally dominant culture in which Christianity provides one dimension of a distinctive worldview. The notion of a 'clash of civilizations' – with the rival groups defined in large part by religious heritage – derives from such an idea. While there is historical resonance in the notion of Christendom, it is not at all evident that Christianity is a defining feature of the West, even as seen from the outside. Indeed, the common epithet used by conservative Muslims is 'godless'. Whether viewed from East Asia or the Islamic world, the Atlantic powers seem characterized most obviously by secular individualism, not by a distinctive religion.

Are we Christian?

From time to time a debate is launched over whether Britain is, or should be, a Christian country. Just what this phrase might mean is exceedingly unclear. In a survey conducted for the Independent Broadcasting Authority in 1987, 38 per cent of respondents said that it was 'very important' for Britain to be a Christian country, with another 31 per cent calling it 'quite important'.[17] It is interesting that at a time when over two-thirds of the population apparently felt national identification as Christian to be important, levels of infant baptism were heading for new lows. The disquieting thought arises that 'Christian' is being used at least by some as a code for 'white', a tendency that the 2001 census question might encourage.

It is perhaps unsurprising that far-right groups are interested in co-opting the term 'Christian', as well as flags and other national symbols. There is no need for anyone else to acquiesce. We must nevertheless recognize a dangerous opportunity for equivocation presented by our question. Britain is still a Christian country in some respects: our general notions of right and wrong, for example, owe at least as much to Jesus as to Jeremy Bentham. It would be illegitimate, however, to see the popular approval of gospel ethics (liberally interpreted) as licence for the ethnocentric proposals that tend to march under the 'Christian country' banner. A desire to preserve the established church does not translate into a vote against planning permission for a Hindu temple. Britain's Christian character is far too complex and nuanced for the label to serve any political purpose beyond sloganeering.

In any case, the question for the longer term is whether this residual sense of Christendom can persist. Long after active participation has ceased, people may still want services for special occasions; after even that degree of interest has waned, they may still accept association with the religion. The result could be described as 'longing-belonging', similar to a self-description as working class by the owner of multiple Jaguars, or claims to Irishness by Americans who have a grandparent from Galway. Such notions of personal identity may well be meaningful, but the chances of passing them successfully to the next generation are not high.

Secularization, on the standard definition, is the process by which religion loses its social significance. A corollary of social significance is importance to personal identity; if life chances depend on clan, class, or creed, then those characteristics will be essential to our sense of who we are. As the significance of such qualities fades, they become more incidental to how we define ourselves. Up to this point changes are hard to measure: most of us can still say where we grew up or what our fathers did, even if no employer or potential spouse is likely to be overly concerned. As ascribed or achieved characteristics lose their social significance, though, they may ultimately disappear from our self-description. Being a Muslim currently seems sufficiently salient that very few British Muslims would not describe themselves as such; for relatively few 'Christians' is the same true.

In a recent paper[18] I suggested that adults appear increasingly unwilling to associate themselves with a denomination unless reinforced by a similarly labelled spouse; adherence otherwise seems deviant. Attachment to the more general category of 'Christian' may follow the same path. At least at present, religious affiliation does not enjoy the exotic glamour of class or ethnic identity, to be claimed from whatever distance. Britain, in short, may still be Christian in some sense, but its identity is increasingly secular.

NOTES

1. Brierley, P. (ed.), *UK Christian Handbook Religious Trends No. 3 – 2002/2003*, Table 2.23.4.
2. Hadaway, C. K. and others, 'What the polls don't show'.
3. As reported in Brierley, P., *The Tide is Running Out.*
4. Hadaway, C. K. and Marler, P. L., 'Did you really go to church this week?'
5. Davie, G., *Religion in Britain since 1945: Believing without Belonging.*
6. Gill, R. and others, 'Is religious belief declining in Britain?'
7. Spencer, W., 'Are the stars coming out?'
8. Davie, *Religion in Britain since 1945.*
9. Gill and others, 'Is religious belief declining in Britain?'; see also the *Tablet* (18 December 1999), p. 1729.

10. I use 'christening' as synonymous with baptism.
11. Voas, D., 'Intermarriage and the demography of secularization'.
12. The *Observer* (1 October 2000), quoting *OK!*
13. Davie, *Religion in Modern Europe*, p. 71.
14. See Brierley, *UK Christian Handbook Religious Trends No. 3 – 2002/2003*.
15. 'Responses to the question would help provide information which would supplement the output from the ethnicity question by identifying ethnic minority sub-groups, particularly those originating from the Indian sub-continent, in terms of their religion.' (*The 2001 Census of Population*, Cmd 4253, 1999, Section III para. 64).
16. As discussed in the previous section, fewer than half of British subjects living in England have had an Anglican baptism. In Scotland and Wales the proportion is much lower. If we exclude children, however, the higher level in England roughly balances the non-Anglicanism of the other countries. The Soul of Britain Survey conducted for the BBC in 2000 produced results broadly consistent with the BSA. Only 48 per cent identified themselves with a faith group (down from 58 per cent in 1990), of whom the Church of England again accounted for a slight majority (25 per cent, as against 40 per cent in 1990). Rather oddly, in view of the relatively low affiliation figure, 23 per cent claimed to attend worship at least once a month, which is higher than most current estimates and other survey findings.
17. Svennevig, M. and others, *Godwatching*, p. 21.
18. Voas, 'Intermarriage and the demography of secularization'.

REFERENCES AND FURTHER READING

Brierley, P., *The Tide is Running Out: Results of the English Church Attendance Survey 1998*. London, Christian Research, 2000.

Brierley, P. (ed.), *UK Christian Handbook Religious Trends No. 3 – 2002/2003*. London, Christian Research, 2001.

Brown, C., *The Death of Christian Britain: Understanding Secularisation 1800–2000*. London, Routledge, 2001.

Bruce, S., *God is Dead: Secularization in the West*. Oxford, Blackwell, 2002.

Davie, G., *Religion in Britain since 1945: Believing without Belonging*. Oxford, Blackwell, 1994.

Davie, G., *Religion in Modern Europe: A Memory Mutates*. Oxford, Oxford University Press, 2000.

Davie, G., *Europe: The Exceptional Case*. London, Darton, Longman and Todd, 2002.

Gill, R., Hadaway, C. K. and Marler, P. L., 'Is religious belief declining in Britain?' in *Journal for the Scientific Study of Religion* 37:3 (1998), pp. 507–16.

Hadaway, C. K., Marler, P. L. and Chaves, M., 'What the polls don't show: A closer look at US church attendance' in *American Sociological Review* 58 (1993), pp. 741–52.

Hadaway, C. K. and Marler, P. L. 'Did you really go to church this week?' in *The Christian Century* (6 May 1998), pp. 472–5.

Spencer, W., 'Are the stars coming out?' in Davie, G., Woodhead, L. and Heelas, P. (eds), *Predicting Religion: Christian, Secular and Alternative Futures*. Aldershot, Ashgate, 2003.

Stark, R., 'Secularization RIP' in *Sociology of Religion* 60 (1999), pp. 249–73.

Svennevig, M., Haldane, I., Spiers, S. and Gunter, B., *Godwatching: Viewers, Religion and Television*. London, John Libbey, 1988.

Voas, D., 'Intermarriage and the demography of secularization' in *British Journal of Sociology* 54 (2003), pp. 83–108.

Wilson, B., *Religion in the Secular Society*. London, Watts, 1966.

8

Mind the Gap: Generational Change and its Implications for Mission

Martyn Percy

Introduction: A short history of change

One the whole, you don't hear of many clergy boasting about the number of older people they have in church, Sunday by Sunday. It would a rare thing to meet a priest who, sitting comfortably at a Chapter Meeting with fellow clergy, sat back and waxed lyrically about the rising number of pensioners that were now attending his or her church. Such bragging, were it to take place at all, would be read by most as a trope of some sort, or perhaps interpreted as a kind of wistful sardonic irony that was trying to make some other point. This may immediately strike one as being rather odd when one considers that many churches are actually (but quietly) rather good at attracting the older person. Older people give time, money and expertise to churches. They tend to be its most loyal and constant supporters. But typically, the discussion about the future of church attendance is shaped around anxieties relating to the young:

> Young people are important members of the Church today, and they also hold the future in its hands. This future is by no means certain. To quote just one statistic, churches lost 155,000 teenagers between 15 and 19, from 1979 to 1989, a loss far greater than the decline of 15 to 19 year olds in the general population.[1]

There are good reasons for these types of anxieties being expressed, to be sure. Concerns about young people and the church are perfectly legitimate missiological issues that need to be addressed. But having said that, one might note that the work of the church with the young has a curiously brief history. True, in the 'golden age' of pastoral ministry (from the Reformation through to the beginning of the Industrial Revolution), many parish priests catechized the young as part of their priestly duties, although there was no particular or specialized outreach to young people worthy of note. George Herbert (1593–1633), for example, advises that children be admitted to Holy Communion as soon as they can distinguish between ordinary bread and consecrated bread, and when they can recite the Lord's Prayer: he estimates the age at which these things come together to be at around seven. Similarly, Parson Woodforde (1740–1803), whilst clearly showing an awareness of young people in his parish, has nothing remarkable to offer them in his ministry.

But lest this sound too complacent, the advent of the Industrial Revolution caused many parents to begin to dread Sundays. As the only day that was free of the toil of the factories (in which the children also worked a six day week), church services became increasingly rowdy. With traditional village and rural ties broken, the 'new generations' of children were also less likely to be inducted into any kind of religious instruction or church custom, and there was general concern about the lapse of the young into crime and delinquency. In Gloucester, England, Robert Raikes (1735–1811), the owner and printer of the *Gloucester Journal*, decided to establish a 'Sunday School' for the children of chimney sweeps, housed in Sooty Alley, opposite the city gaol. The School began in 1780, and was an immediate success, offering general and religious education to children from the working classes. The idea of the schools spread with astonishing rapidity. By 1785 a national Sunday School Organization had been established, and many thousands of children were attending in most major cities.[2] In 1788 John Wesley wrote: 'verily I think these Sunday Schools are one of the noblest specimens of charity which have been set on foot in England since William the Conqueror'.

Sunday Schools continued to spread and develop throughout the nineteenth century, with their aims and objectives altering in the course of their evolution. By 1851, three-quarters of working class children were in attendance, and many adults too.[3] In Raikes' original scheme, social action and evangelization had been the primary motivation in the formation of the schools. Yet by the mid-1800s, some scholars assert that the primary focus of the Sunday School had become a means of expressing emergent working class values (e.g. thrift, communalism, self-discipline, industry, etc). In other words, the Sunday Schools had become a means of providing some generational continuity and identity. Moreover, the 'associational' character of the Sunday Schools also provided a significant social environment in which young and old, male and female, could meet and interact. Thus, Joseph Lawson, writing in the 1890s, notes:

> Chapels are now more inviting – have better music – service of song – which cannot help being attractive to the young as well as beneficial to

all. They have sewing classes, bazaars, concerts, and the drama; cricket
and football clubs, and harriers; societies for mutual improvement and
excursions to the seaside.[4]

Lawson's observations from over a century ago are illuminating because
they draw our attention to the fecund associational nature of Victorian
religion. Indeed, this lasted, in all probability, well into the twentieth
century, with religious bodies providing significant social capital, the means
whereby malevolent and anti-social forces were overcome by the purposeful
encouragement of 'mutual support, cooperation, trust, institutional
effectiveness'.[5] Religion, in its many and varied associational forms and
offshoots, provided social capital that was both bridging (inclusive across
different social groups, trans-generational, gender-encompassing, etc.) and
bonding (exclusive – clubs and societies for particular groups, boys' clubs,
girls' clubs, etc.), and was therefore part of that new social culture which
now obviated the generational gaps that had first awoken the reformers of
the early nineteenth century. But the mid-twentieth century was to mark
further changes for the churches. As Putnam notes of North America, in the
1950s roughly one in every four Americans reported membership with a
church-related group, but by the 1990s that figure was cut in half to one in
eight. Americans now devote two-thirds less of their time to religion than
they did in the 1960s.[6]

What has led to this change? There is a variety of theories that offer
'generational change' in religious affiliation as a way of framing the causes
and trajectories, and the insights, although of a fairly general nature, are
useful. Putnam, for example, states that

> The decline in religious participation, like many of the changes in
> political and community life, is attributable largely to generational
> differences. Any given cohort of Americans seems not to have reduced
> religious observance over the years, but more recent generations are less
> observant than their parents. The slow but inexorable replacement of
> one generation by the next has gradually but inevitably lowered our
> national involvement in religious activities.[7]

For Wade Clark Roof and William McKinney, the transition is marked by
movement from formal religious observance and membership to 'surfing'
from congregation to congregation, not belonging strongly to any one
particular body of believers, and an increased appetite for spirituality:

> Large numbers of young, well-educated middle-class youth[s]...
> defected from the churches in the late sixties and seventies ... Some
> joined new religious movements, others sought personal enlightenment
> through various spiritual therapies and disciplines, but most simply

'dropped out' of organized religion altogether... [there was a] tendency toward highly individualised [religion] ... greater personal fulfilment and the quest for the ideal self ... religion [became] 'privatised' or more anchored to the personal realms.[8]

We might add to these observations a remark from Margaret Mead, that 'the young cannot learn in the old ways' and that 'the old are outmoded rapidly' in the speedily advancing and saturated world of media, science, questing and consumerist cultures.[9]

Speaking of culture, we might also mention Callum Brown's *The Death of Christian Britain*, in which he argues that the very core of the nation's religious culture has been irrevocably eroded. More unusually, however, he argues that the process known as 'secularization', whilst gradual and endemic, is not the industrial revolution or the enlightenment. Rather he argues that it is the catastrophic and abrupt cultural revolutions of the post-war years, and most especially those trends and movements that began in the 1960s.

Charting the growth of institutional religion in Britain from 1945 to the early 1960s, Brown contends that it is the change in the role of women that has done for Christianity, rather than scientific rationalism. The apparent feminization of religion in the Victorian led to a resurgence of family values in post-war Britain, in which various bourgeois standards rose to the surface, and were equated with 'religion' (e.g. Sabbath observance, drinking in moderation, etc.). What undid this cultural trajectory was a combination of liberalism and feminism – Brown cites The Beatles and the end of the ban on *Lady Chatterley's Lover* as examples. Brown's book is full of insight, and his appeal to cultural forces of late modernity as a corrosive influence on religious adherence have far more nuance than those that are normally to be found amongst the pages of secularization theorists:

> It took several centuries (in what historians used to call the Dark Ages) to convert Britain to Christianity, but it has taken less than forty years for the country to forsake it. For a thousand years, Christianity penetrated deeply into the lives of the people, enduring Reformation, Enlightenment and the industrial revolution by adapting to each new social and cultural context that arose. Then really, quite suddenly in 1963, something very profound ruptured the character of the nation and its people, sending organised Christianity on a downward spiral to the margins of social significance. In unprecedented numbers, the British people have stopped going to church ... The cycle of intergenerational renewal of Christian affiliation, a cycle which had for so many centuries tied the people however closely or loosely to the churches and to Christian moral benchmarks, was permanently disrupted in the 'swinging sixties'. Since

then, a formerly religious people have entirely forsaken organised Christianity in a sudden plunge into a truly secular condition.[10]

Brown's assertions appear to confirm the underlying thesis that we have so far been sketching in this opening section, namely that large-scale disaffection with organized religion is primarily a post-war phenomenon in both Britain and America. Furthermore, the changes are due to broader cultural streams that the churches have no direct control over. These cultural changes might include the rise of the 'post-associational' society, consumerism, individualism, an accentuation of generational identity and familial atomization. However, it is important not to allow such descriptions to become the only frames of reference for determining reality. To this end, some problems with the historical narrative are worth pointing out.

First, it needs to be remembered that our ways of talking about generations – especially childhood – do not have fixed points of meaning. Historians of childhood often quip that a child over the age of seven in medieval times did not exist. The term 'teenager' and the very idea of adolescence are comparatively recent 'discoveries'. The emergence of a 'buffer zone' of development between childhood and adulthood is something that is mostly attributable to economic and social conditions that can afford such space for maturity and advancement. The cultivation of such a zone as an arena for further specific forms of consumerism only serves to concretize and consecrate such identities. (Today, in many developing countries, a 'child' of 10 can be the main 'bread-winner'.) Before the onset of the industrial revolution in Western Europe, it should be recalled that the churches could not claim to be doing any special work with children. As Heywood points out, prior to 1800, there was 'an absence of an established sequence for starting work, leaving home and setting up an independent household'.[11] Indeed, it is only the child labour laws and schooling that provide 'age-graded' structures for social ordering at this level, and such provisions are less than two hundred years old. Often, the work of churches went hand in hand with educationalists, and a newly perceived need to provide 'nurseries of Christian character' at every 'stage' of childhood, from infancy through to the age of twenty, in order to advance civilization and good social ordering.[12]

Second, generational change in religious adherence does not necessarily mean the rise of secularization. Brown, for example, cites 1963 as the beginning of the end for the churches. So how long would it be before Britain becomes 'truly' and wholly secular? Brown does not say, but the teasing question draws our attention to his rhetoric, which contain in-built vectors of decline: 'ruptured', 'downward spiral', 'disrupted', 'forsaken' and 'sudden plunge' suggest a mind already made up. Whilst it may be true that the sixties, with its revolutions of popular culture, social liberalism and political upheaval did more to question and shake the foundations of institutions than in previous generations, it would appear that Brown is also guilty of shaping his facts around his thesis. Whilst it is clearly helpful to assess religious adherence down the ages through the lens of generational change, it simply does not follow that if the present generation are uninterested in religion or spirituality, then the next will be even less so. Moreover, is it not the case that many religious movements began in the 1960s? Ecumenism, charismatic renewal, the New Age movement and a variety of sects, cults and new religious movements were part and parcel of a culture of experimentation that dominated the 1960s. Would it not be fairer to say that, far from turning off religion, people were rather turned on by it, and tuned into it in new ways (e.g. spirituality) that simply reflected the emerging post-institutional and post-associational patterns of post-war Britain?

Third, far from seeing generational change as a threat to the churches, the cultural forces that shape debates should be seen in the wider context of general social change. In a capitalist and consumerist culture, it is probably reasonable to go along with Putnam's hypothesis that the late twentieth century has seen a dramatic collapse in many forms of civic association, and a corresponding rise in individualism. However, churches have tended to hold up rather well under this pressure when compared to their non-religious counterparts. That said, changes in the way people spend 'free' time does appear to have had a deleterious effect on associational forms, and in all probability no agent of change has been more influential than the television. Initially, the creation of the 'electronic hearth' was a family-bonding and generation-bridging experience. But as consumerism and individualism has steadily increased, this phenomenon has changed. In the USA, the average adult now watches almost four hours of TV per day. As the number of television sets per household multiplies, watching programmes together has become more rare. Television has evolved into an example of 'negative social capital'; it is the new public space through which the world speaks to us, but it means that we no longer talk to one another. Putnam points out that 'husbands and wives spend three or four times as much time watching television as they spend talking'.[13] Similarly, Putnam points out that 'unlike those who rely on newspapers, radio and television for news ... Americans who rely *primarily* on the internet for news are actually *less* likely than their fellow citizens to be civically involved'.[14] But of course, this does not mean that technology spells the end for civic life, associations and religious adherence. Rather, it suggests a new mutation of social and religious values, and it is to the discussion of this that we now turn.

Generations and mission

Every generation that has ever lived has done so within its own modernity. Each new generation that faces its past, present and future does so with a sense of being on the cusp of time. Continuity between generations may be valued; but it is also evaluated as it is appreciated, and then perhaps subjected to alteration. But how true is it that the cultural and social forces being addressed at the present are more problematic than those faced in the past? Can it really be said that the transformations of the late twentieth century are more disruptive than those experienced in the Industrial Revolution, or in the wake of the economic and social re-ordering that followed the Black Death in medieval England? In general, it would be imprudent to argue (historically) that one generation has struggled more than another, and that the forces shaping religion and society are now more or less inimical than another period. It is important that in any sociological and cultural analysis, proper attention is paid to (proper) history, before engaging in any kind of speculative futurology. There is a well-known aphorism that needs heeding by every would-be cultural commentator: 'sociology is history, but with the hard work taken out'. To avoid the endemic sociological habit of generalizing, it is important that any discussion of the generations is rooted in a sound grasp of historical enquiry, and, where possible, married to data, ethnography and other forms of intellectual garnering that are rooted in methodological rigour. Two examples are offered here that paint slightly different pictures. The first is a Roman Catholic and North American perspective, and the second is a British one.

Roman Catholics in the third millennium are a diverse body of believers, and the relationship between 'official' and 'operant' in American Catholic religion is under increasing academic scrutiny:

> Most observers agree that there is a great deal of diversity among American Catholics ... While there was a certain amount of diversity in the 1940s and 1950s ... the beliefs and practices of American Catholics have become increasingly varied since then. Studies done during the 1950s and 1960s indicated that there was more uniformity among Catholics than among mainstream Protestant groups ... More recent research, however, suggests that American Catholics' beliefs and practices are now more diverse than they were prior to the Second Vatican Council.[15]

Williams and Davidson, in their study of American Catholicism, offer a generational explanation for the seismic shifts of the last fifty years. The pre-Vatican II generation (born in the 1930s and 40s) viewed the church as an important mediating force in their relationship with God. When asked why they were Catholic, many participants in the Williams and Davidson study replied that it was because 'it was the one true church'. The Vatican II generation (born in the 1950s and 60s), however, were more circumspect about the nature of the church and its absolutist claims. Interviewees were more inclined to see their priest as representing 'official' religion, which, in turn, was only one religious source that fed and nurtured their private and individual spirituality. In this sense, the Vatican II generation is pivotal, since the post-Vatican II generation (born in the 70s and 80s) has tended to be even more liberal and open. For this generation, Mass attendance is not a priority; being a good person is more important than being a good Catholic; faith is individualistic and private – 'what really counts is what is in your heart'. Davidson and Williams conclude their study with these words:

> One thing is certain: the hands of time cannot be turned back. Societal changes, as well as changes occurring within the church, leave no doubt that tomorrow's Catholics will be very different from previous generations. The children of post-Vatican II Catholics will receive their religious education from those who never read the *Baltimore Catechism*, and are likely to know little about the changes brought about by Vatican II. The conceptions of faith post-Vatican II Catholics are apt to pass on to the next generation will look decidedly individualistic in nature.[16]

In a similar vein, Sylvia Collins bases her assessment about the future shape of spirituality and youth on just such foundations. Her research is not motivated by confessional or denominational anxiety, but is rather located in the quest to discover how young people are changing in their attitudes to belief. Contrasting 'baby boomers' (those born between 1945 and 1960) and 'baby busters' (those born after 1960), Collins skilfully notes and narrates the changes between the generations. On balance, 'boomers' tended towards radicalizing religious traditions in the wake of post-war settlement. This was to include an emphasis on liberation, justice and political involvement, but was also coupled to an increasing tendency to experiment with religion (e.g. innovative 'sects', New Religious Movements, Communitarianism, etc.). Thus, the

> baby boomer generation ... saw spirituality among young people move in line with social change from its location in one main tradition associated with the old established order, through to a new spirituality that sought to break the bonds of establishment and set the self free to reach its new potential. Even more widespread, however, was a

growing apathy and indifference towards the spiritual realm altogether in favour of materialistic self-orientation in terms of hedonistic consumption.[17]

Collins argues that 'baby busters' followed up and extended these changes. She notes, in common with other sociologists such as Hervieu-Léger, Walker, Francis and Kay that the late twentieth century has seen 'a thorough-going fragmentation in lineage of Christian memory', that 'gospel amnesia' has set in, as society has come to observe the fragmentation of belief and decontextualization of spirituality. But lest this sound too pessimistic already, Collins points out that religion has merely mutated rather than disappeared:

> Spirituality ... has moved from the self-spirituality of the boomer generation to a more aesthetic spirituality, a spirituality which is focused on pleasure and experience in and of itself ... Successful churches, it seems, offer an atmosphere and intimate experience of God over and above doctrine ... the spirituality of intimacy of the millennial generation will be deeply bound up with the consumerism that has increasingly concerned youth throughout the post-war period.[18]

Collins' analysis is persuasive on many levels; her descriptive arguments appear to be a good 'fit' for young people and spirituality at the dawn of a third millennium. However, one important caveat should be mentioned, namely that of change. Interest in, or even a passion for, 'an intimate experience of God over and above doctrine' is not necessarily sustainable over a period of time. It does not follow that those things that are valued and cherished in teenage years or one's early twenties will even be regarded in one's 30s or 40s. For example, many young people are enchanted by the discipline, fellowship and spiritual atmosphere of a Christian Union while at college or university. But large numbers of students will quietly forsake this type of commitment for a different *attitude* to belief in later years: something altogether more mellow, temperate, open, ambiguous – a faith that can live with doubt.

This transition from the early twenties into 'young adulthood' raises some intriguing issues for the consideration of generations. Wade Clark Roof notes that 'in times of social upheaval and cultural discontinuity especially, generations tend to become more sharply set off from one another'.[19] The added power of consumerism in late modernity reinforces this sense: niche marketing to almost every age group for every stage of life is not only prevalent, but also highly successful. And in the early years of adulthood, the desires appear to be less clustered around fulfilment and more around authenticity. As Parks notes, there is a 'hunger for authenticity, for correspondence between one's outer and inner lives ... a desire to break through into a more spacious and nourishing conception of the common life we all share.[20] Parks' work is one of the few treatments of faith and belief in the 'twenty-something' age group, and her work is a prescient consideration of how generational change evolves within itself, even to the point of questioning the contemporary bewitchments of consumerism and self-fulfilment.

The idea that changes take place *within* generations, and not simply between them, is an important one to grasp in the consideration of the future of religion, spirituality and the churches. Personal and communal beliefs have to be sufficiently robust to cope with all stages of life (if they are to last), and they also need the capacity to be able to negotiate the standard ruptures in mundane reality that raise questions about meaning and value. Such occurrences are typically located in the traditional turning points of life such as birth, death and marriage.[21] And of course, as has been implied throughout this essay, cultures themselves can undergo rapid changes that make adaptation essential, particularly for institutions, with which we are also concerned.

The idea of churches adapting to culture is as old as the hills. There is no expression of ecclesiology that is not, in some rich and variegated sense, a reaction against, response to or attempted redemption of its contextual environment. Churches may choose to regard themselves as being primarily for or against culture (following Niebuhr), but as I have recently argued,[22] what mainly characterizes ecclesial responses to culture is their *resilience*, either in the form of resistance or accommodation, but, more usually, by combining both in its strategic survival and mission within late modernity. This observation is important here, for it reminds us that religion is both deeply part of and also totally apart from culture. Its sheer alterity is what gives it its power, as much as it is wholly incarnated within space, time and sociality. In other words, religion is that material which generations will attempt to fashion and shape around their needs and desires. But the power of religion will also fashion and shape its 'users', causing them to question, reflect and wonder. Religion evokes awe; the numinous inspires; the spiritual invites a quest of ceaseless wandering.

That said, many theological, ministerial and ecclesial responses to the rapid cultural changes of late modernity, coupled to the apparently dynamic differentiation between generations, has caused the spilling of much ink. Christian bookshops are awash with literature on how to reach the young, how to engage with secular culture, and how to reach those who are 'spiritual but not religious'. Typically, the character of these works is conditioned by a general sense of panic and fear, with churches engaging in ever more neuralgic responses to the perceived crisis: flight, fright and fight would not be too wide of the mark. This is especially true in the arena of 'popular culture', where, ironically, spiritual motifs, symbols and ideas are plentiful: one trips over such 'cultural furniture' all the time in the somewhat haphazard assemblage of late modern life. There are, of course, more sophisticated attempts to read 'the signs of the times', and come up with compelling and thoughtful responses to the apparent 'generation gap'.

Paul Abrecht, for example, offered a serious theological and ecclesiological programme for the churches that was prescient for its time – the crucible of the early 1960s. More tangentially, Milton Rokeach provides a way of understanding how human values are translated and learnt from one generation to the next, and from group to group within institutions. Indeed, there is now an abundance of works that could be at the service of the churches, helping them to read cultural and generational change.[23] But on the whole most theologians ignore such tasks, leaving the arena free for smaller confessional voices to shout and narrower tribal interests to be developed.

So far, I have deliberately avoided mentioning postmodernity – the name for the 'condition' that many of the present generation are supposed to be labouring under. I have chosen this path because I do not think it is especially useful to add further characterization to the present debate. Of course, I am prepared to concede that there are aspects to postmodern reflection that are appropriate and analytically descriptive for our purposes here. For example, I find that Lyotard's quip that postmodernity is essentially 'incredulity at metanarratives' to be an apt encapsulation of our political, social and civic times. It is true that attitudes to truth have shifted too, but this does not appear to mean that Western civilization is about to collapse, or that my grandparents' generation will have proved to be more truthful than that of my children. It is also true that belief systems – for individuals and institutions – more often than not resemble a new assemblage and collage than any strict continuity with tradition. But at the same time, no one can convincingly prove that this situation for society is new, namely a morass of competing convictions, and that pluralism is particular to late modernity. It isn't. From earliest times, Christians have carved out their faith in a pluralist world, settled churches in alien cultures, and adopted their practices and customs that have eventually become 'tradition'.

I suspect that the litmus test for assessing the extent of generational change and its implications for mission can probably be best understood by speculating about death and memorialization in the future. If our cultural commentators – who speak of 'gospel amnesia' and 'a thorough-going fragmentation in lineage of Christian memory' – are right, then what will a funeral look like in fifty years' time? At present, many ministers conducting funerals can be confident that, unless otherwise requested, there will be Christian hymns and prayers at the ceremony. The Lord's Prayer may be said, and is still mumbled by many in traditional language. Some hymns – a number of which were learnt at school – can be sung, and it is just possible that certain passages of scripture and collects will be familiar to a number of the mourners. But what of the future, where prayers, collects and hymns are not likely to have been part of the schooling for the vast majority of mourners? What types of religious sentiment will be uttered by the generation that is, in all probability, non-conversant in the language of formal religion, but fluent in the many dialects of spirituality?

To partly answer my own question, I turn to an analogy drawn from the world of art history. Restorers of paintings sometimes talk about the 'pentimento', the original sketch that is underneath an oil painting beginning to show through as the painting ages. The pentimento is a kind of skeletal plan (the first lines drawn on canvas): where paint falls or peels off, the earliest ideas for the picture are sometimes revealed. The analogy allows us to pose a question: what will the spiritual pentimento of today's children look like when it comes to their funeral? It will, I suspect, at least at a church funeral, be primarily Christian, provided we understand the term 'Christian' broadly. It will be a kind of vernacular, operant (rather than formal), folk Christianity, not that dissimilar from what many ministers already encounter. But it will also be a more spiritually open and evocative affair, with perhaps readings from other traditions. It will also be more therapeutic, centred less on grief and more on celebration. In all likelihood, the funeral of the future will be able to tell us just how much change there has been between the generations. There will be gaps, to be sure, but they are unlikely to be unbridgeable. Previous generations have always found a way through to the next; there is no reason to suppose that this generation will lack the wisdom and the tenacity to do likewise. After all, etymologically 'religion' comes from two Latin words, meaning 'to bind together'.

Futurescape:
Opportunities and challenge for the churches

In this brief and final section we can do no more than suggest some further avenues for exploration. It is a fact that generational change and its implications for mission is an under-researched area, and that the churches, with what research data is available, have been reluctant to read and react.

As we have already indicated, this is probably motivated by fear as much as anything else. Churches are afraid of what David Ford terms 'the multiple overwhelmings of modernity', and this then characterizes their responses to rapid social change and the apparently inexorable rise of popular and consumerist culture. And yet as we have seen, in the midst of these conditions, spirituality appears to thrive, although there is apparently now a greater gap between formal religion and the beliefs and values (operant religion) of the present generation. Having said that, it must be remembered that beliefs and values are not fixed in generations or between them; change is here to stay. With these remarks in mind, there are five points to make by way of conclusion.

First, Putnam's analysis of the 'post-associational' society raises some intriguing missiological questions for the churches as they seek to shape their ministry. Similarly, Grace Davie's well-known mantra 'believing without belonging' has been used to characterize British churchgoing habits since 1945, and the statistical data tend to bear out her thesis. The question for the churches is, therefore, how they can operate in a climate where people accept the message but don't respond with commitment? Of course, *insisting* on commitment is one way forward, but it is unlikely to be enough. Increasingly, churches will have to accommodate a society that expects and demands a reflexivity in its patterns of belonging. Moreover, it is likely that churches will have to provide associational opportunities for a society that marked by diversity and mobility, and is less concerned with territoriality. This shift can be characterized as a move from the dispositional to the episodic. Whereas parochial or local churches once assumed that they operated within fairly settled and identifiable communities, these same churches will now have to work for the many different (and sometimes transient) groups within the community. This will demand more creativity, tenacity and flexibility in local mission, and less stress on the apparent 'givenness' of a community.

Second, Putnam's work might also lead us to question the extent to which churches are too broad in their appeal. Although a number of evangelical churches and other Christian traditions have enjoyed consider-able success with 'family worship', there may also be room for specific services and meetings that target particular ages. There is nothing new here: pram services, Sunday Schools and the like have been held for more than a century. But churches may need to put more energy into considering how they appeal to individuals in their 20s and 30s who may not have families, to those who have retired from work, and to other niche groups. With the increasing atomization of the generations within society, churches can swim with the culture as well as acting counter-culturally. They can meet specific generational needs (bonding), but also provide environments for generational bridging. But again, this will need to be done in a social landscape where diversity and mobility are increasing, and where people may belong to several different places and interact with a multiplicity of communities.

Third, churches need to see that the debate about how to minister to the generations is not best served by the old 'traditional-progressive' or 'conservative-liberal' divides. Heywood's history of childhood shows us, for example, that when history is done properly, it shows that feminism has not eroded the traditional status of mothers. Many mothers had a miserable time in eighteenth and nineteenth century industrial Britain; rates of bastardy were high, as were those of neglect, abandonment and infant mortality. Mothers had to work to survive; orphanages were filled to overflowing when either one or both parents could not work, or there was economic decline. The generation of 'stay at home wives' whose sole duty was to care for their children is but a brief blip on the landscape of social history, at least in Western Europe and North America. The churches can help understanding across generations by not siding with one against another, but by educating each successive generation into properly understanding how they have come to be (e.g. values, beliefs, ideals, etc.), and how it might live out the gospel in its own time.

Fourth, if the history of generations and the churches is done properly, we can also see that the churches' 'success' with the young is relatively brief, and is also linked to wider social and civic aspirations. This is important, for children often mean different things to different con-gregations: they symbolize something to present generations, and this is often subject to change. For some, children are a sign of spiritual strength and fecundity. Others display them in worship prominently, and others 'school' them quite apart from the church (and quietly).[24] But lest this sound too *laisser-faire*, the churches will have to work harder to reach each new generation, because, if Brown is right, the 'cycle of inter-generational renewal' has indeed been disrupted in late modernity. We cannot assume that our children will want, do, believe or behave as we have. No one can afford to be complacent. But no one should be overly pessimistic either.

Fifth, there are still certain occasions that reach across the generations, of which religion is likely to remain an intrinsic part. To return to funerals, we can see this most clearly at times of national disaster – the funeral of Diana, Princess of Wales; the memorialization surrounding the attacks in Washington and New York on 11 September 2001; the outpouring of vernacular spiritual grief for the victims of Hillsborough, Heysel or almost anywhere else one can think to mention. At such times, the churches can often provide an inclusive act of supra-memorialization which bridges the generations, unites in grief and hope, and expresses the latent prayers and spiritual pentimento of a people that want to be together when it matters most. It is here, in these situations, that the churches must continue to reflect on how they provide the *something* that is much more than 'something for everyone'. For it is in these moments that generational gaps are bridged, wounds healed and shared understandings and memories begin to emerge, surpassing those particularities that are specific to ages and groups. It is at this point that some kind of creativity and hope is produced for each new generation. Finally, there is something we can all talk about; something that we can all recollect and locate ourselves through; there is something to pass on; and something to shape the future.

NOTES

1. Collins, S., 'Spirituality and Youth', p. 221, quoting Brierley, P., *Act on the Facts*, p. 214.
2. Kelly, T., *A History of Adult Education in Liverpool*, pp. 74–6.
3. Laqueur, T., *Religion and Respectability*, p. 44.
4. Cunningham, H., *Leisure in the Industrial Revolution*, p. 181.
5. Putnam, R., *Bowling Alone*, p. 22.
6. Putnam, *Bowling Alone*, p. 72.
7. *Bowling Alone*, p. 72.
8. Roof, W. and McKinney, W., *American Mainline Religion*, pp. 78, 1819, 323.
9. Mead, M., *Culture and Commitment*, p. 78.
10. Brown, C., *The Death of Christian Britain*, p. 1.
11. Heywood, C., *A History of Childhood*, p. 171; see also Goldscheider, F. and C., *Leaving Home before Marriage*.
12. Kett, J., *Rites of Passage*.
13. Putnam, *Bowling Alone*, p. 224.
14. *Bowling Alone*, p. 221.
15. Williams, A. and Davidson, J., 'Catholic Conceptions of Faith', p. 70.
16. Williams and Davidson, 'Catholic Conceptions of Faith', p. 75.
17. Collins, 'Spirituality and Youth', p. 229.
18. 'Spirituality and Youth', pp. 233–5.
19. Roof, W., *A Generation of Seekers*, p. 3.
20. Parks, S., *Big Questions*, pp. 9–16.
21. See the titles by Goldscheider and Kett listed in References and Further Reading.
22. Percy, M., *Salt of the Earth: Religious Resilience in a Secular Age*.
23. See for example the titles in References and Further Reading by Hall and Neitz, Strinati, Thompson and Zaltman.
24. See Hopewell, J., *Congregation*, p. 8.

REFERENCES AND FURTHER READING

Abrecht, P., *The Churches and Rapid Social Change*. London, SCM Press, 1961.

Brierley, P., *Act on the Facts*. London, Marc Europe, 1992.

Brown, C., *The Death of Christian Britain: Understanding Secularisation 1800–2000*. London, Routledge, 2000.

Cunningham, H., *Leisure in the Industrial Revolution*. Beckenham, Croom Helm, 1980.

Collins, S., 'Spirituality and Youth' in Percy, M. (ed.), *Calling Time: Religion and Change at the Turn of the Millennium*. Sheffield, Sheffield Academic Press, 2000.

Francis, L. and Kay, W., *Teenage Religion and Values*. Leominster, Gracewing, 1995.

Goldscheider, F. and C., *Leaving Home Before Marriage: Ethnicity, Familism and Generational Relationships*. Wisconsin, University of Wisconsin, 1993.

Hall, J. and Neitz, M., *Culture: Sociological Perspectives*. New Jersey, Prentice Hall, 1993.

Hopewell, J., *Congregation: Stories and Structures*. London, SCM Press, 1987.

Hervieu-Léger, D., *Religion as a Chain of Memory*. Cambridge, Polity, 2000.

Heywood, C., *A History of Childhood: Children and Childhood in the West from Medieval to Modern Times*. Cambridge, Polity, 2001.

Kelly, T., *A History of Adult Education in Liverpool*. Liverpool, Liverpool University Press, 1970.

Kett, J., *Rites of Passage: Adolescence in America, 1790 to the Present*. New York, Basic Books, 1977.

Laqueur, T., *Religion and Respectability: Sunday Schools and Working Class Culture 1780–1850*. New Haven, Yale University Press, 1976.

McLeod, H., *Secularisation in Western Europe 1848–1914*. London, Macmillan/Palgrave, 2000.

Mead, M., *Culture and Commitment: The New Relationships Between the Generations in the 1970s*. New York, Doubleday, 1978.

Parks, S., *Big Questions, Worthy Dreams: Mentoring Young Adults in Their Search for Meaning, Purpose, and Faith*. San Francisco, Jossey-Bass, 2000.

Percy, M., *Calling Time: Religion and Change at the Turn of the Millennium*. Sheffield, Sheffield Academic Press, 2000.

Percy, M., *Salt of the Earth: Religious Resilience in a Secular Age*. Sheffield, Sheffield Academic Press, 2002.

Putnam, R., *Bowling Alone: The Collapse and Revival of American Community*. New York, Simon and Schuster, 2000.

Rokeach, M., *Understanding Human Values: Individual and Societal*. New York, Free Press, 1979.

Roof, W., *A Generation of Seekers: The Spiritual Journeys of the Baby Boom Generation*. San Francisco, HarperCollins, 1993.

Roof, W. and McKinney, W., *American Mainline Religion: Its Changing Shape and Form*. New Jersey, Rutgers University Press, 1987.

Strinati, D., *Popular Culture: An Introduction to Theories*. New York, Routledge, 1995.

Thompson, M. and others (eds), *Cultural Theory*. Boulder, Westview Press, 1990.

Walker, A., *Telling the Story*. London, SPCK, 1996.

Williams, A. and Davidson, J., 'Catholic Conceptions of Faith: A Generational Analysis' in *Sociology of Religion*. 57:3 (1996).

Zaltman, G., *Processes and Phenomena of Social Change*. New York, Wiley, 1973.

9

The State of Faith

Paul Avis

One of the major concerns underlying this volume is a missiological one – the need for correct information on which a reliable interpretation of the spiritual dimension of our culture, the context of mission, can be based. It is pretty unarguable that the Church's mission (that is to say, of course, the Church's role in the mission of God, *missio dei*) needs to be focused. Obviously it will not be effective if its energy is dissipated in a random, untargeted way. Casting your bread upon the waters, as Ecclesiastes 11.1 enjoins, is all very well provided you know where the relevant waters are. Effective outreach is informed and focused by knowledge of its object. The need for empirical, particularly statistical, research in the service of mission is now generally recognized by the churches. However, three main difficulties arise when we attempt to harness sociological research in the service of mission.

The first problem is that research projects are often not commensurable, they do not easily match up. They tend to ask different questions. They often ask those questions of different constituencies. And they ask them for different purposes. They cannot always be compared in order to arrive at a more complete picture. They are not straightforwardly cumulative: you cannot simply add them together.

The second difficulty is that researchers who design empirical projects are not always theologically skilled (though some are highly competent theologically). Their questions about religious belief are usually lacking in refinement and are sometimes crude and inept.

The third issue is that the interpretation of the answers that researchers receive is sometimes rather rough and ready. It can be a blunt instrument in the hands of the more journalistic forms of religious survey. Interpretation is a theological as well as a sociological matter. Interpretation cannot be read off in a value-free way, as though the data spoke for itself. We need to tread much more carefully in this area than some pundits tend to do.

I am going to attempt to put together a broad picture of the current state of religious awareness and affiliation – to assess the state of faith – in a way that overcomes some of these difficulties. I hope to achieve an analysis that is more robust than some in two respects.

- First, I cast my net fairly widely, taking into account a broad range of religious surveys, conducted over a protracted period of time, on religious belief and affiliation, so that they are allowed to supplement and correct one another where that is feasible.
- Second, I evaluate critically some of the theological issues that are implied in the questions that are frequently asked in questionnaires and interviews.

The empirical surveys on which I draw are:

- The European Value Systems Study Group Research carried out in 1985 and again in 1990.[1]
- The survey of Religion and Television in Great Britain carried out in 1987 (TVR) and a similar project undertaken in 1993.[2]
- The British Social Attitudes Surveys of 1991 and 2000/2001.[3]
- The general surveys of British habits, attitudes and beliefs conducted by MORI in 1989 and Gallup in 1985.[4]
- The Rural Church Project of 1990 (RCP), though this survey, being confined to rural areas, does not provide an analysis that is representative of the population as a whole.[5]
- The interview-based research into inner-city religious beliefs and attitudes carried out in Tower Hamlets by Geoffrey Ahern in 1985.[6]
- The long-term research into young people's attitudes to Christianity carried out by Leslie Francis.[7]
- The comprehensive synthesis and interpretation of empirical studies relating to belief, ethical stance and habits of churchgoing, provided by Robin Gill.[8]

I am also aware of three rather broad-brush surveys, timed to coincide with the millennium celebrations, that appeared as I was completing this study:

- First, Gallup International's Millennium Survey 'Religion in the World at the end of the millennium'. Conducted in sixty countries world wide, this is too general to be helpful for our purposes, though its figure of 20 per cent for western Europeans attending a religious service at least once a week does provide a useful benchmark against which to measure practice in Britain, which is thought to be around 10 per cent.[9]

- Second, the Opinion Research Business survey (A), summarized in *The Tablet* for 18 December 1999. This shows a marked decline in Christian profession between 1957 and today, though the methodology indicated in the article seems insufficiently precise to justify the managing director Gordon Heald's opening remark that 'only a minority of Britons now believe in the tenets of Christianity'. His conclusion is not borne out by the evidence that I will deploy below. In this survey, six per cent of respondents declared themselves to be convinced atheists. This figure, though higher than that of other surveys, is still only one tenth of the proportion of respondents who believed in either a 'personal God' or a spirit, God or life force.
- Third, the survey of 1,000 people conducted by Opinion Research Business (B) for the BBC to launch its series *Soul of Britain* after Easter 2000 (*The Tablet*, 3 June 2000). This significantly shows an increased interest in general spiritual matters (with a small rise in the numbers of people who believe they have a soul). However, my confidence in this survey is considerably dented by the garbled question on church and state which refers to the Church of England as the established church for *Britain* (the Church of Scotland, the established church north of the border, will not take kindly to that). I also have other methodological concerns that I will come to shortly.

The 'dumbing down' of survey questions in these latest exercises is disturbing. Opinion Research Business (A) wanted to test what proportion of respondents believed that Jesus was the Son of God. The metaphor of divine sonship, though biblical and credal, is inadequate if it is taken as the sole indicator of belief in the deity of Jesus Christ. However, at least the terms of the question were identical in 1957 and 1999. One alternative answer offered was not identical. A 'fictional story' in 1957 became 'just a story' in 1999. Perhaps it was thought that some people would not know what 'fictional' meant. But 'just a story' is ambiguous and confusing because at one level, the gospel narrative is of course a story and the difference between a story and 'just a story' is unacceptably opaque.

I also note that in both the Gallup and the Opinion Research Business (A) surveys, the category of 'agnostic' ('I do not know whether there is a God') was equated to 'I don't know what to think'. This is completely unsatisfactory. Not knowing what to think is very different from being clearly convinced, like the classical agnostic, that I do not know the answer or that the answer is not available to us. Some notable Victorian agnostics knew exactly what they thought. Those who say they do not know what to think may be just confused. It would not be surprising if, in this new millennium period of flux and transition, large numbers, especially of young people, were very uncertain about their beliefs. Perhaps this explains why Opinion Research Business puts the proportion of those who do not know what to think at 16 per cent, while MORI in 1989 found just 4 per cent were agnostic. In what follows, I shall show that various other survey formulations are theologically crude and inadequate. To organize the data, I borrow Grace Davie's useful distinction between believing and belonging.

Believing

Our starting point must be the consensus of polls that show that between two-thirds and three-quarters of the population of Britain 'believes in God' after a fashion, including those who waver and those who believe in a higher power (76 per cent in MORI 1989; 70 per cent in Gallup 1985; 71 per cent in the European Values Survey 1990; 62 per cent in Opinion Research Business (B) 2000; 72 per cent in British Social Attitudes 2000/2001). About 4 per cent are convinced atheists, while another 4 per cent are agnostic (MORI).

The British Social Attitudes Survey of 1991 appeared to register atheism at 10 per cent, agnosticism at 14 per cent and various degrees of belief in God or a higher power at three-quarters of the population.[10] However, there are two problems concealed in these figures. The first problem concerns the discrepancy in the percentage of atheists in the two surveys. The second has to do with the discrepancy between the statistics for belief that there is a God and for belief *in* God respectively.

Let us take the issue of atheism first. Bruce points out that, in the BSAS 1991, of the forty-five persons who claimed not to believe in God (not 'there is no God', as Bruce paraphrases it, which is a rather different matter, as we shall see immediately), twenty claimed a denominational attachment, ten believed in some sort of spirit or life force, ten believed in life after death and one even believed in a personal God![11] Taking out those groups reduces the number of consistent atheists to around four per cent, which tallies more or less with other evidence. But this remains an extraordinary discrepancy in the presentation of data.

The discrepancy is compounded in the latest BSAS.[12] Here there appears to be no category for convinced atheists. The nearest approximations are, 'I don't believe in God now and never have,' and 'I don't believe in God'. The negative statement, that one does not believe in God, does not equate to the positive statement, that there is no God, and cannot be made to do duty for it. Moreover, the question on agnosticism conflates two propositions that do not necessarily stand or fall together: 'I don't know whether there is a God and I don't believe there is any way to find out'. Not being in a position to know oneself whether there is a God may be an expression of a number of attitudes and states of mind: humility, confusion, doubt. It is not by any means the same as the dogmatic affirmation that the question is inherently unanswerable.

Now let us turn to the issue of how the question of belief in God is phrased. It seems to make a difference whether people are asked (a) if they believe *in* God, or (b) if they believe that God exists or that there is a God.[13] These two questions, sometimes conflated, are actually categorically or qualitatively different and the consequences for our understanding of common religion are profound. They have importantly different connotations. Though the surface grammar may seem innocuous, the depth grammar is highly significant. As Dr Anne Richards has noted (in a personal comment to me), some people with a fragile sense of self-worth will say they do not believe in God when what they mean is that they do not believe that God can believe in them. The difference between the two questions explains the discrepancy between two statistics: 96 per cent believe that God exists, or at least do not deny it, but only 75 per cent are able to say that they believe in God.

The fact that the overwhelming majority of the population accepts, with greater or lesser degrees of conviction, that some kind of God exists is impressive. We might be tempted to play down the significance of these figures, however, by suggesting that they measure merely nominal or notional belief rather than deep conviction. In his *Essay in Aid of a Grammar of Assent* (published in 1870) John Henry Newman distinguished between *notional* and *real* assent and claimed that the majority of English Protestants merely gave notional assent to Christian beliefs. In traditionally Catholic countries like Spain, by contrast, Newman believed, assent to religious objects was real not notional. 'To them the Supreme Being, our Lord, the Blessed Virgin, Angels and Saints, heaven and hell, are as present as if they were objects of sight; but such a faith does not suit the genius of modern England.' English Protestantism, Newman continued, consists of little more than reading the Bible and leading a moral life, combined with a firm grasp of the doctrine of divine providence.[14]

Newman's analysis is of course dated (I imagine that few nominal Christians are regular Bible readers nowadays) and his distinction between notional and real assent must take context into account. It is likely, on the face of it, that there is a proportion of nominal or notional belief in God concealed in the statistics that we are considering. But we are surely held back from devaluing the belief of the vast majority who believe in God by the fact that 42 per cent of people claimed to be 'certain' that there is a God (TVR). The British Social Attitudes Survey of 1991 turned up 23 per cent who had no doubts that God exists (here the element of certainty regarding the existence of God approximates this attitude to belief *in* God) and a further 24 per cent who affirmed, 'While I have doubts, I feel I do believe in God'.[15] These figures were very slightly eroded in the 1998 survey, but not so as to be statistically significant.[16]

The ambiguity of all questions that ask people for a personal statement about God can be highlighted from the angle of Wittgensteinian philosophy. Norman Malcolm has questioned whether one could believe, in any meaningful sense, that God exists without actually believing in God, even believing in a God whom one feared or loathed. Given the unique content of the word 'God' in a Judaeo-Christian culture, to believe that God exists without having some affective attitude towards God is logically, as well as psychologically, impossible. 'If one conceived of God as the almighty creator of the world and judge of mankind how could one believe that he exists, but not be touched *at all* by awe or dismay or fear?' A belief that God exists, concludes Malcolm, if it were logically independent of any and all ways of regarding God, 'would be of no interest, even to God'.[17] The ambiguity of the question must surely lead to ambiguity in the data that we cannot unravel now. Given that all questions about God are fraught with personal agenda, it would be helpful if future surveys did not ask the particularly loaded question, 'Do you believe *in* God?'

What kind of God do people 'believe in'? Here the issue of what is meant by 'a personal God' rears its head. Extraordinarily, BSAS 1998 gave individuals the opportunity to say that they did *not* believe in a personal God, but not that they *did* believe.[18] EVS found that only one third believed in a 'personal God'.[19] But probably too much weight should not be put on this proportion. The term 'personal God' is not only theologically sophisticated but is also inherently ambiguous. It could be taken in a theologically acceptable sense to mean that God is a being who is not less than personal, by analogy with human personhood. But it could also be taken, in an acceptable sense, to mean that 'God is personal to me'. In a culture where everything valuable has to be customized or personalized, it could even have connotations of 'my personal God', by analogy with 'my personal fitness trainer' or even 'my personal stereo'.

The less ambitious (though not less theologically eye-brow-raising) formula that God is 'a person', employed by TVR, elicited 37 per cent agreement. In both surveys (EVS and TVR) about 40 per cent thought of God as an impersonal power, spirit or life force. However, when this was explicitly contrasted with belief in a personal God by BSAS, the proportion who profess belief in 'a Higher Power of some kind' – though not in a personal God – has consistently registered only 13 or 14 per cent.[20] Christian theology would have considerable difficulty with any claim that God was impersonal. But to think of God as Spirit is – or may be – perfectly orthodox and is compatible with the personal nature of God.[21] Moreover, to picture God as a life force, while theologically deficient from a Christian point of view, is close to the more immanental images of God that have become more salient in Christian theology in the past century: God as Presence, as Friend, as Healer, as Mother, as Other.

It is widely thought that our image of society, our image of the self and our image of God are interrelated or interdependent. Jung argued throughout his writings that symbols of the self and symbols of God are indistinguishable in clinical analysis.[22] Mary Douglas has pinpointed the correlation between images of self and images of society. The confluence of these insights points to the tendency of images of society, self and God to reflect one another. It is probable that shaping influences (I do not say determinative influences), arising from the conjunction of economic, social and psychological factors in a given society, results in a fundamental common structure of images for those aspects of existence to which we award supreme moral and sacred value.

On this premise, Dobbelaere argues that, in an increasingly impersonal society, belief in a personal God becomes increasingly problematic. 'How could he be thought of as a "personal" God if people experience fewer and fewer "personal" relationships in their public life? For a society in which impersonal, segmented role relations prevail, belief in a personal God ... seems an anachronism.'[23] This reflection suggests to me that, given that people's image of God is subject to influences that are not under their personal control, we should be more tolerant when people attach the tag 'impersonal' to their notions of God and that we should not dismiss them from a Christian point of view. At the same time, however, we should of course work for a society in which personal relationships are nurtured and privileged and it may well be that, as a result, people will be helped to think of God in a more adequate way. In these relatively unfavourable circumstances, Christian apologetics could start from the insight that, as the source of all personhood, God not only cannot be less than personal but must also transcend any notion of personhood that we may arrive at.

According to TVR, 62 per cent of people believe in God as creator and 47 per cent believe that God knows all that they do and think. In the British Social Attitudes surveys of 1991 and 1998 only 30–32 per cent disagreed with the proposition that 'There is a God who concerns himself with every human being personally' – roughly the same proportion that agreed with the proposition.[24] The two questions (about God's knowledge and about God's care) are not strictly commensurable: one concerns what theologians or philosophers would call a metaphysical attribute of God (God's omniscience); the other concerns a moral attribute (God's care or love). Nevertheless, these figures could suggest that a larger proportion of the population believes in the Judaeo-Christian form of theism than is indicated by the figures showing belief in a personal God or God as a person at about one in three. It may be that a significant proportion of the population is sophisticated enough to shy away from a too overtly anthropomorphic conception of God as a 'person'.

We may well wonder, however, whether research in the *inner city* would suggest a different, a less encouraging picture. It is significant that the consensus is not challenged by Ahern's findings in Tower Hamlets. When asked whether they believed in God, Ahern's interviewees did not appear to distinguish between theism and pantheism (though they would not have used those technical terms). Neither did they bring up issues of 'creation, omnipotence, omniscience, human free will'. 'It was as if "God" was taken for granted as a word and to *think* about it was strange'.[25] Cox, in his historical study of religion and the churches in Lambeth from 1870 to 1930, identified a similar phenomenon which he called 'diffusive Christianity'. He doubted whether this should be interpreted as a debased form of an earlier pure popular orthodoxy and suggested that it was perhaps 'the most that a millennium of indoctrination had achieved in implanting Christian ideas in the popular mind'. Cox went on to conclude that this 'diffusive Christianity' was 'something more than simple theism, although not much more'.[26] Forster has spoken of the 'residual religiosity' to be found on a Hull council estate where religion had an 'important safety-net function' for most people.[27] To come up to date: Bishop Laurie Green stresses that though 'in the inner city there is a great warehouse full of spirituality ... which is yearning for expression and which the Church is expected somehow to articulate,' it is at heart an unreflective, nonconceptual spirituality.[28]

Turning now to other Christian credal beliefs, TVR found that three quarters of the population believed that Jesus is the Son of God: 45 per cent were certain of this, while 29 per cent thought that it was probably true. Those who consciously rejected this central tenet of the Christian faith were a mere 11 per cent – about one in ten of the population – and this proportion presumably included those of other faiths, particularly Jews and Moslems. In inner-city Tower Hamlets Geoffrey Ahern found that about a quarter of his (white) interviewees believed that Jesus was the Son of God, others having a naturalistic explanation of who Jesus was.[29]

The British Social Attitudes survey of 1991 asked about *belief in life after death*. Less than half of the sample held this belief and a roughly similar proportion believed in heaven.[30] The European Value Systems Survey Group (EVS) found that 43 per cent of the British sample held a belief in life after death (with a marked difference between the beliefs of men (34 per cent) and of women (51 per cent)).[31] The Rural Church Project also explored beliefs about life after death. Only half of the total rural sample had a belief in an afterlife (three-fifths of women and two-fifths of men). A quarter of the sample professed not to know and 28 per cent were convinced that death was the end.[32] In Tower Hamlets about a third believed in life after death, a third disbelieved and a third were agnostic.[33] Belief in life after death is clearly one of the weakest areas of common religious beliefs and it is a little surprising that support for it was not even weaker in an urban survey. However, people's cool and considered opinions are often swept away when their feelings are deeply touched. The outpouring of grief for Diana Princess of Wales and on other similar occasions before and since may tell a different story. When the books of condolence are fully analysed they may cause us to revise our assumption that belief in life after death is the weakest plank of belief as far as common religion is concerned. A good deal depends on how the questions are framed.

The European Values Survey of 1990 shows a slight decline in subscription to Christian beliefs (sin, heaven, hell, etc.) but a rise in interest in the spiritual dimension of life (thinking about the meaning of life and death, for example).[34] This trend seems to be broadly borne out by Opinion Research Business (B) in 2000. Apparently there has been no major erosion of religious belief, though there has perhaps been a slight shift of emphasis. The age and gender variables, on the other hand, show significant differences, with a sharp reduction in religiosity as we move down the age scale and a marked disparity between the religiosity of women and men.[35]

With the possible exception of life after death, there is impressive evidence of the persistence of basic Christian beliefs. Interestingly, however, the role of belief itself, as a component of religion, was only moderately rated. When asked by TVR what was the most important part of religion, half replied, 'What you do to others', but only 37 per cent rated 'What you believe' as the most important. It seems likely that this perspective is also a legacy of Christian influence, for though credal confession plays a significant part in Christian initiation, the influence of Christian teaching has tended to depress propositional beliefs in favour of moral behaviour: 'Religion that is pure and undefiled before God, the Father, is this: to care for orphans and widows in their distress, and to keep oneself unstained by the world' (James 1.27). From the inner-urban context, Ahern comments that it is a mistake to project our educated emphasis on 'belief in belief' into the inner city. He testifies: 'My most lasting impression of white, working-class Tower Hamlets . . . is of the inappropriateness of the cultural concepts of "belief" and "disbelief".'[36] Green points out that 'there is no credal orthodoxy' in the common religion of the inner city and in the way that local people use the church and its rites of passage.[37]

Though the influence of Christian beliefs persists in common religion, there are certainly no grounds for complacency on the part of the churches. The beliefs of common religion are tending to drift further from orthodoxy, they are prone to syncretism and are vulnerable to dissolution. Unless the sense of belonging can be strengthened, beliefs may fade away or mutate into forms that lie ever further from mainstream Christianity. Bruce, though apparently not very sympathetic to the Church's cause, warns that 'individual beliefs which are not regularly articulated and affirmed in a group, which are not refined and burnished by shared ceremonies, which are not the object of regular and systematic elaboration, and which are not taught to the next generation or to outsiders' count for little in the long term.[38]

Belonging

We now turn to the second major variable in religious attitudes, the sense of participating in, identifying with or belonging to a faith, religion or church. The definition of belonging has to be as broad as that in order to accommodate the different criteria of the various surveys. A useful marker is the fact that only 14.4 per cent of the population of the United Kingdom explicitly claim active membership of a Christian church – and this figure should be reduced in order to apply to England as it is inflated by higher active participation in the 'Celtic fringes', most notably Northern Ireland. Davie has summarized the state of church membership thus: 'It is undeniable that the membership of the principal Christian denominations in this country is declining. The rate of this decline is, however, uneven and some denominations have managed – temporarily at least – to arrest this trend altogether. In addition, some of the fall in membership has been offset by the rapid growth in the independent churches and among Pentecostals, and by a steady increase in the Orthodox population'.[39] But, as we shall see straight away, active participatory membership is not a criterion of 'belonging' that would be accepted by many who claim some kind of affiliation to a religion or church. And we also have to take seriously the fact that church 'membership' is not an idea that is much used in the Church of England. Theologically speaking, membership is of the Body of Christ through baptism, not of a denomination, still less of a congregation. The church electoral roll is not a membership list, but has the limited purpose of facilitating church government at every level. The Church of England is interested in maximizing participation and in fostering Christian discipleship, not in keeping lists of paid-up members of a denomination.

In 1989, 88 per cent of people told MORI that they belonged to a Christian church or denomination. The latest research among television viewers shows more than 70 per cent identifying themselves as Christian and of these 40 per cent (a marked drop on earlier statistics) were Anglican, 14 per cent (an increase) were Roman Catholic. Only 22 per cent of the population claimed no sort of religious membership.[40]

Three-fifths of people identified themselves as 'religious' to the European Values Survey (EVS) in 1980, but this was slightly down in 1990. The Television survey (TVR) found that half the population describes itself as 'very' or 'fairly' religious. Gallup discovered that nearly two-thirds of people in Britain saw themselves as religious to some degree, while the latest television research shows 10 per cent of people as very religious, 31 percent as fairly religious and 33 per cent as not very religious – though only a quarter described themselves as not at all religious.[41] The British Social Attitudes survey of 1991 identified 40 per cent of people as seriously religious.[42] If we conflate these figures, the conclusion suggests itself that around half the population of the United Kingdom sees itself as moderately religious or at least definitely sympathetic to religion.

EVS also found that half of the population regularly feels the need for prayer, contemplation or meditation and draws comfort and strength from religion. The same proportion scored above the mid-point on the 'importance of God' scale. In the 1990 survey, interestingly, more people felt the need for prayer but fewer drew comfort from religion or held that God was important in their lives.[43]

About nine per cent of people attend church weekly in Britain as a whole (eight per cent in England), but it is estimated that approximately 19 per cent can be regarded as committed churchgoers if we include those who do not attend weekly. The Church of England has been working recently on ways of obtaining more accurate figures for changing patterns of church-going, including mid-week attendance. Among Roman Catholics, for whom attendance at weekly Mass is an obligation, only about one quarter now complies.[44] Interestingly, only a tiny proportion of the population (3 per cent: TVR) considers that going to church is the most important part of religion. In the late 1980s MORI found that 17 per cent of people claimed to attend a place of worship regularly and a further 22 per cent occasionally. Forty-three per cent attended church for christenings, weddings and funerals only, but a mere 18 per cent said they never went to a church. Gallup, a few years earlier, discovered that 20 per cent of people claimed to attend a religious service at least once a month and another 23 per cent who went occasionally. Recent television research came up with the perplexing figure of 23 per cent (of all faiths) who claimed to attend a religious meeting place at least once a month and another 45 per cent who attended only for special family or other occasions – these are the substantial rump of the 'common religion' constituency.[45] The British Social Attitudes survey found that about half the population visits a church at least sometimes while the other half never does so. It is not clear in most cases whether a visit to the crematorium chapel counts!

The Rural Church Project (RCP) found that the overwhelming majority of the rural population (88 per cent) considers that it 'belongs' to a church, denomination or religion – the emphasis being on belonging to a tradition or community. Considering that church attendance in the countryside is only a fraction of this proportion, it seems clear that what most people see as being religious or belonging to a religion is very different from the way the churches themselves, with their emphasis on 'commitment', understand the matter.

In the inner city, according to Green, there is still a strong emphasis on locality and belonging and the church is expected to be part of the landscape, but the idea of attending a church service is utterly alien to most inner-city residents. It does not follow, however, either that they do not have any kind of faith or that they feel that the church is nothing to do with them. 'A lack of overt religious activity among the white indigenous folk does not mean that they have no faith, but that in comparison with other faiths, Western-style Christianity has not offered them an easily-expressible outward sign of belonging. There is no special costume to wear, no special prayer to make, no distinctive food to eat.'[46] Green points out that, although the need to belong to a community is becoming more desperate in our increasingly fragmented society, the opportunity to belong is becoming more intangible and elusive. 'It is not believing and doctrine but belonging which is the key to transcendent experience in the inner city. UPA [Urban Priority Area] people believe in belonging – belonging to a place, to one another and to God.'[47]

Francis and Kay, researching among young people, have used a criterion – attitude to Christianity – that does not fit neatly under the headings of either believing or belonging. However, their findings give cause for concern. They indicate a 'consistent and persistent decline in attitude towards Christianity throughout the whole age range'.[48] Overall, this decline was pronounced between 1974 and 1986 but has since levelled off. The Christian faith has ceased to be taken seriously by many young people and religion seems to be regarded as on a par with music as an area of study that is not deemed relevant to adult life and the pursuit of a career.[49] Negative attitudes to Christianity are also creeping down the age range so that attitudes prevalent among school leavers twenty years ago are now common among those in the middle years of secondary education.[50] On the other hand, as we shall see immediately, there is impressive evidence of religious experience among young people.

The community constraints – the social glue – that reinforced churchgoing have lost their strength. To attend is now almost entirely an individual decision. Bruce writes (with some hyperbole, it must be said): 'Church attendance has now become so rare in Britain that it is no longer supported by group pressure and is no longer an important mark of "belonging" to any larger social formation. It has become an almost purely personal or idiosyncratic matter.'[51] At the end of his analysis of the secularization thesis, with detailed reference to Lambeth in the period 1870 to 1930, Cox suggests that the combination of religious broadcasting, with its substantial audiences, and religious education in schools, came to serve as a substitute for active church participation and 'sustains a "diffusive Christianity" in England even as the churches wither away'.[52]

Finally under the heading of belonging, I want to mention one of the most disturbing statistics I have come across in this piece of research.[53] It concerns individuals' attitudes to the Church: specifically, whether they trust the Church. EVS 1990 shows that only 43 per cent trust the Church. Half of all women but only a third of all men trust the institution. Among young people (18–24), only 30 per cent trust it. The Church has about the same rating as the civil service and somewhat less than the educational system (47 per cent). It has almost half the trust-rating of the armed services (81 per cent). In the Soul of Britain survey (2000), the church had slipped further behind these institutions and levelled out at 37 per cent.[54] Recent scandals about sexual abuse by the clergy can only serve to depress this proportion further. The loss of people's trust in the Church must surely rank as one of the greatest of all impediments to mission. It would be extremely useful to know why the Church scores so abysmally. The strategy that is called for in response is one that places a high priority on the building of trust between the Church and individuals, the Church and communities.[55]

Conclusions

In this chapter I have argued that, in order to carry out its mission in the world in an intelligent and effective way, the Church needs the resources that expert empirical study of religious belief and practice can provide. An attempt to synthesize a wide range of findings shows that adherence to some central tenets of Christian belief is still strong and goes deep, even though that adherence does not translate into an equivalent commitment to participate in the organized life of the churches. Elsewhere I have argued that the rapport with the Christian faith and the receptivity to what the Church has to offer, on the part of the general population, is much greater than either church leaders or media pundits are inclined to assume. On this basis I have advocated a strategy for the pastoral mission of the Church.[56]

I have argued here, however, that the usefulness of some current empirical work is hampered by its incommensurability with other similar studies and even by internal inconsistency in the framing of questions over time. I have pointed out that a degree of theological sophistication is required in both the drafting of questions and the analysis of the answers. This theological awareness is not always in evidence. The body of empirical material that is currently available is flawed by lack of theological sensitivity. Both questions and interpretations are sometimes marked by crudity and lack of nuance. Sensitivity to what may underlie people's responses is called for because there are cultural constraints on the ways that people think and express themselves on matters of belief – for example, concerning gendered and personalist language about God. I have also suggested that a degree of tolerance and flexibility, informed by pastoral empathy, is appropriate when people express their beliefs in forms that are not exactly central to the Christian tradition – for example, when they speak of God as a life force. Finally, I have highlighted some evidence of a crisis of trust with regard to the church as an institution – so basic to the success of the Church's pastoral mission – and pointed to the need for strategies of committed engagement that over time might remedy this disturbing situation.

NOTES

1. Abrams, M. and others, *Values and Social Change in Britain*; Timms, N., *Family and Citizenship*; Barker, E. and others (eds), *Secularization, Rationalism and Sectarianism*; cf. Davie, G., *Religion in Britain since 1945*.
2. Svennevig, M. and others, *Godwatching*; Gunter, B. and Viney, R., *Seeing is Believing*.
3. The 1991 survey is analysed in Greeley, A., 'Religion in Britain, Ireland and the USA' and summarized in Bruce, S., *Religion in Modern Britain*; for the 2000/2001 survey, see Jowell, R. and others (eds), *British Social Attitudes, the 17th Report, 2000/2001 edition*.
4. Jacobs, E. and Worcester, R., *We British*; Heald, T. and Whybrow, R., *The Gallup Survey of Britain*; summary in Gunter and Viney, *Seeing is Believing*.
5. Davies, D. and others, *Church and Religion in Rural England*.
6. Ahern, G. and Davie, G., *Inner City God*.
7. Summarized in Kay, W. K. and Francis, L. J., *Drift from the Churches*.
8. Gill, R., *Churchgoing and Christian Ethics*.
9. http://www.gallup.international.com/survey15.htm
10. Greeley, 'Religion in Britain, Ireland and the USA'.
11. Bruce, *Religion in Modern Britain*.
12. Jowell and others (eds), *British Social Attitudes, the 17th Report, 2000/2001 edition*, p. 125.
13. Cf. Greeley, 'Religion in Britain, Ireland and the USA', p. 67.
14. Newman, J. H., *An Essay in Aid of a Grammar of Assent*, pp. 55f.
15. Cf. Greeley, 'Religion in Britain, Ireland and the USA'.

16. Jowell and others (eds), *British Social Attitudes, the 17th Report, 2000/2001 edition*, p. 125.
17. Malcolm, N., 'Is it a Religious Belief that God Exists?', pp. 106ff.
18. Jowell and others (eds), *British Social Attitudes, the 17th Report, 2000/2001 edition*, p. 125.
19. Timms, N., *Family and Citizenship*, p. 69.
20. Jowell and others (eds), *British Social Attitudes, the 17th Report, 2000/2001 edition*, p. 125.
21. John 4.24: 'God is spirit'. Cf. Lampe, G. W. H., *God is Spirit*.
22. Cf. Avis, P., *Faith in the Fires of Criticism*, pp. 97ff.
23. Barker and others (eds), *Secularization, Rationalism and Sectarianism*, p. 26.
24. Jowell and others (eds), *British Social Attitudes, the 17th Report, 2000/2001 edition*, p. 126.
25. Ahern and Davie, *Inner City God*, p. 109.
26. Cox, J., *The English Churches in a Secular Society*, p. 95.
27. Forster, P. G., 'Residual Religiosity on a Hull Council Estate', p. 25.
28. Sedgwick, P. (ed.), *God in the City*, p. 78.
29. Ahern and Davie, *Inner City God*, p. 112.
30. Greeley, 'Religion in Britain, Ireland and the USA'.
31. Timms, *Family and Citizenship*, p. 69.
32. RCP IV, pp. 222ff.
33. Ahern and Davie, *Inner City God*, p. 112.
34. See Davie, *Religion in Britain since 1945*, p. 78.
35. Davie, *Religion in Britain since 1945*, pp. 118ff.
36. Ahern and Davie, *Inner City God*, p. 80.
37. Sedgwick, *God in the City*, p. 88.
38. Bruce, *Religion in the Modern World*, p. 58.
39. Davie, *Religion in Britain since 1945*, pp. 47, 49.
40. Gunter and Viney, *Seeing is Believing*, pp. 11ff.
41. *Seeing is Believing*, pp. 11ff.
42. Greeley, 'Religion in Britain, Ireland the USA'.
43. Abrams and others (eds), *Values and Social Change in Britain*; Davie, *Religion in Britain since 1945*, p. 78.
44. *The Times* (3 January 1998).
45. Gunter and Viney, *Seeing is Believing*, pp. 11ff.
46. Green, in Sedgwick (ed.), *God in the City*, p. 75.
47. Green, in *God in the City*, p. 87.
48. Kay and Francis, *Drift from the Churches*, p. 5.
49. *Drift from the Churches*, pp. 30–1.
50. *Drift from the Churches*, p. 42.
51. Bruce, *Religion in Modern Britain*, p. 44.
52. Cox, *The English Churches in a Secular Society*, p. 276.
53. Timms, *Family and Citizenship*, p. 130.
54. Heald, G., 'The Soul of Britain'.
55. See further Avis, P., *A Church Drawing Near*.
56. Avis, *A Church Drawing Near*.

REFERENCES

Abrams, M., Gerard, D. and Timms, N., *Values and Social Change in Britain*. London, Macmillan, 1985.

Ahern, G. and Davie, G., *Inner City God*. London, Hodder and Stoughton, 1987.

Avis, P., *Faith in the Fires of Criticism*. London, Darton, Longman and Todd, 1995.

Avis, P., *A Church Drawing Near: Spirituality and Mission in a Post-Christian Culture*. Edinburgh, T. & T. Clark/Continuum, 2003.

Barker, E., Beckford, J. A. and Dobbelaere, K. (eds), *Secularization, Rationalism and Sectarianism: Essays in Honour of Bryan R. Wilson*. Oxford, Clarendon Press, 1993.

Bruce, S., *Religion in Modern Britain*. Oxford, Oxford University Press, 1995.

Bruce, S., *Religion in the Modern World: From Cathedrals to Cults*. Oxford, Oxford University Press, 1996.

Cox, J., *The English Churches in a Secular Society: Lambeth, 1870–1930*. New York and Oxford, Oxford University Press, 1982.

Davie, G., *Religion in Britain since 1945: Believing without Belonging*. Oxford, Blackwell, 1994.

Davies, D., Watkins, C. and Winter, M., *Church and Religion in Rural England*. Edinburgh, T. & T. Clark, 1991.

Douglas, M., *Natural Symbols*. London, Cresset Press, 1970.

Forster, P. G., 'Residual Religiosity on a Hull Council Estate' in Forster, P. G. (ed.), *Contemporary Mainstream Religion: Studies in Humberside and Lincolnshire*. Aldershot and Brookfield VT, Avebury, 1995.

Gallup International, *Religion in the World at the End of the Millennium*. www.gallup-international.com/survey15.htm.

Gill, R., *Churchgoing and Christian Ethics*. Cambridge, Cambridge University Press, 1999.

Greeley, A., 'Religion in Britain, Ireland and the USA' in Jowell, R., Brook, L., Prior, G. and Taylor, B. (eds), *British Social Attitudes: The Ninth Report*. Aldershot and Brookfield VT, Dartmouth Publishing, 1992.

Gunter, B. and Viney, R., *Seeing is Believing: Religion and Television in the 1990's*. London, John Libbey, 1994.

Heald, G., 'Taking Faith's Temperature' in *The Tablet* (18 December 1999).

Heald, G., 'The Soul of Britain' in *The Tablet* (3 June 2000), pp. 770–1.

Heald, T. and Whybrow, R. J., *The Gallup Survey of Britain*. London, Croom Helm, 1986.

Jacobs, E. and Worcester, R., *We British: Britain under the MORIscope*. London, Weidenfeld and Nicolson, 1990.

Jowell, R. et al. (eds), *British Social Attitudes, the 17th Report, 2000/2001 edition*. London, Sage (National Council for Social Research), 2000.

Kay, W. K. and Francis, L. J., *Drift from the Churches: Attitude Toward Christianity During Childhood and Adolescence*. Cardiff, University of Wales Press, 1996.

Lampe, G. W. H., *God as Spirit*, Oxford, Oxford University Press, 1977.

Malcolm, N., 'Is it a Religious Belief that God Exists?' in Hick, J. (ed.), *Faith and the Philosophers*. New York, St Martin's Press, 1964.

Newman, J. H., *An Essay in Aid of a Grammar of Assent*. London, Longmans, Green, 1903.

Sedgwick, P. (ed.), *God in the City: Essays and Reflections from the Archbishop's Urban Theology Group*. London, Mowbray, 1995.

Svennevig, M., Haldane, I., Spiers, S. and Gunter, B., *Godwatching: Viewers, Religion and Television*. London, Libbey, 1988.

Timms, N., *Family and Citizenship: Values in Contemporary Britain*. Aldershot, Dartmouth Publishing, 1992.

Acknowledgement: I am most grateful to the Revd Lynda Barley, head of the Church of England's Research and Statistics department, for helpful comments on an earlier draft of the paper, but I take responsibility for the contents as they stand.